The Treasured Collection of Golden Heart Farm
A Biography of
Wilhelmina Weber Furlong (1878-1962)
and her beloved
Thomas (Tomas) Furlong (1886-1952)

Clint Bernard Weber

The Weber Furlong Collection Publishing Company

The Weber Furlong Foundation

Marfa, Texas, Alpine, Texas, New York, New York

Bolton Landing, New York; Glens Falls, New York

weberfurlong.com

Revised First Edition

Library of Congress Cataloging in Publication Data

Clint B. Weber

The Treasured Collection of Golden Heart Farm

A Biography of

Wilhelmina Weber Furlong (1878-1962)

and her beloved

Thomas (Tomas) Furlong (1886-1952)

ISBN 978-0-9851601-0-4

Copyright © 1898-2012 by Clint B. Weber

Foreword by: James K. Kettlewell, Professor Emeritus, Skidmore College, Saratoga Springs, NY

Dedicated to Bernard E. Weber III

The cover photo of Thomas & Weber Furlong would become the symbol of Golden Heart Farm for this biography. Shown are August C. Weber, Thomas Furlong, and Wilhelmina Weber Furlong.

Weber Furlong and the Modern Style

Weber Furlong produced paintings of such quality that she should be numbered among the important artists of her time. Unfortunately, she remains largely unknown outside of the Glens Falls area, though her name often occurs in art historical accounts of the many significant artists whom she knew, among them Rockwell Kent, Thomas Hart Benton, Alexander Calder, Max Weber, and of course David Smith. So, it is not as if Weber Furlong did not have networking contacts with the art world. These were the years when her close friend David Smith was emerging as a success, and very probably she attended a number of affairs where leading critics such as Clement Greenberg and Robert Coates were present.

It is my observation that Weber Furlong effaced herself as an artist during the years when her husband Thomas Furlong was alive. As a painter, he was not very good, and she probably recognized this. She only emerged as an artist after his death in 1952. And at that time the only art that could make it in America had to be very large and very abstract. Nevertheless, the art she produced was entirely of her time.

Weber Furlong painted only still-lifes. This is quite unusual. Very few artists in art history specialized so exclusively in still-life painting. And yet, it is the quintessential subject of Modern Art. Modern Art (with capital letters) was a style dominated by what we now call "formalism." The formalist doctrine holds that design, the compositional structure, is the essential prerequisite for anything that is to be considered art. It is what allies the visual arts to music and dance. It follows that the purest art form would be pure design, and therefore completely abstract.

Since the time that the French eighteenth-century painter Chardin created major works of art through arrangements of objects so common and ordinary that their only value was in the arrangement itself, still-life painting has been a vehicle for emphasizing the design side of art. Cezanne carried Chardin's tradition into the modern age. The generation of artists to which Weber Furlong belonged all looked back to Cezanne as the great form giver of Modern Art.

In the twentieth century, when Picasso and his Cubist associates developed Synthetic Cubism as a style based purely on formal relationships, still-life became their primary subject matter. It is this tradition to which Weber Furlong's paintings belong. And, like Picasso, and like the first generation of Modern Artists in America, her art never became entirely abstract. Rather, she sought out a compromise between abstract and representational forms.

In her still-life painting, Weber Furlong began as a formalist, creating patterns with objects. In her style, she followed Cezanne's system of intensified seeing, in which complex formal patterns are uncovered through a careful analysis of one's visual perceptions. As she evolved, Weber Furlong became more and more engaged in the objects themselves. As she explained to me in a number of the conversations we had about her art in the late 1950s and early 1960s, she had now found in the things she painted almost human personalities and emotions. The expression of feeling in her art had become as important to her as design. Such sensitivity to the expressive content of form is normally associated with the expressionist rather than the formalist side of Modern Art. Expressionism, an artistic tendency which ran parallel to formalism in the twentieth century, placed emphasis on the emotional effects of shapes, colors, and brushwork. So, as Weber Furlong's style evolved, there occurred a convergence of expressionism and formalism, the two principal lines of development of

Modern Art. This was during the 1950s, when a similar convergence occurred in the New York School paintings of Jackson Pollock, Willem De Kooning, and Franz Kline.

As her style continued to evolve, she added to these still-life objects, selected now for their expressive shapes, an ever more focused and intense color. In this, she was following a traditional idea in art that color contacts directly the observer's emotions. (Form, on the other hand, is supposed to appeal to the reasoning part of the mind.) So, with the increase of the color intensity of her work, the emotional content increased. Consistent with this, her brushstrokes became ever more strong and expressive (and personal). As the color and brushstroke became more important, the objects in her still-lifes became more simple. In these developments, her artistic motives and painting style came to ally her work closely to Abstract Expressionism, which many of us think of as the great climax of the Modern Art movement. If, as we hope, Weber Furlong ultimately finds the place she and her art deserve in the art historical record, she will be classified with the Abstract Expressionists, as was her friend, the greatest sculptor of the American Modern movement, David Smith.

The greatness of Weber Furlong's late work has to do with precisely why it is eminently Modern. In it we see an intensification of the formalist concern for achieving a visual beauty through form and color; pattern-making always lies at the core of a true Modern Art style. But now, Weber Furlong's brilliant arrangements are suffused with human feelings.

James K. Kettlewell
Professor Emeritus
Skidmore College
Saratoga Springs, NY

Preface

Marfa, Texas 2012-2013

This is the story of the life of Wilhelmina Weber Furlong, a major American artist who pioneered modern impression-istic and still-life painting at the turn of the twentieth century's modernist movement. The story includes the life of her husband Thomas Furlong, a well-known muralist, and art teacher.

Reconstructing the forgotten history of Wilhelmina Weber, which I undertook in 2011, through my explorations of the collections of Golden Heart Farm has certainly transformed my life. It seemed to me Wilhelmina's work had been lost to the world, and I had initially planned to refer to her work as "The Lost Collection." However, my mother was quick to point out that we had always known its location. It is time to bring her work, and her remarkable life story to the forefront. She was an amazing woman, who deserves recognition for her accomplishments, and her contribution to the history of American Art.

The biography, retrospective catalogue, and exhibition of artwork, are a presentation set up to preserve the life works of Wilhelmina Weber Furlong and tell her story. This retrospective of paintings is the collection of her personal works and the works of avant-garde artists of the time, who interacted with her on a regular basis throughout their lives. Personal writings and belongings are included in the Weber Furlong Collection to give visitors a more personal experience.

In 2012, the Weber Furlong Foundation's collection of her art and personal belongings from Golden Heart Farm was organized for its first public viewing in Marfa, Texas at the International Woman's Foundation historic Building 98 from September 27, 2012 through February 15, 2013.

The museum exhibit fully recreated the artist studio and bedroom of the 1920s, featuring the belongings that remain from the Golden Heart Farm. Building 98 stands in a large historic U.S. Cavalry fort that was operational during the Spanish-American War through World War II, which includes the Mexican Revolution, when Miss Weber was in Mexico City. Paintings were exhibited in the officers' quarters and in the officers' ballroom. The lectures and presentations took place in the officer's library and the event reception in the officer's club and dining hall, a regular stop of Colonel George Patton during the Mexican Revolution. Dignitaries from the Texas State Historical Commission attended and volunteers were lining up to help. People from all over the country wanted to be involved with the amazing history presented for the groundbreaking début of this historic collection. Her evocative biography is a result of her fascinating life story. Family accounts and saved correspondences, as well as firsthand community accounts, are part of the history. Without the help of those who knew Wilhelmina Weber, this narrative would not have been possible.

The high-definition documentary "Wilhelmina Weber Furlong" compiled from these events will undoubtedly continue to bring this narrative to the forefront. The filming of oral histories began in Bolton Landing, New York and in Glens Falls, in May of 2012, and continued to the International Woman's Foundation exhibition in Marfa, Texas at Building 98. The following year, in late June of 2013, the oral history interviews resumed in Manhattan, and Plattsburgh, New York, with the assistance of the Clinton County Historical Association, a point of contact for the North Country project was established. Then on Tuesday, July 23, 2013, the Glens Falls Common Council approved the placing of a New York State historical marker in the landscaped area in front of the city's Ridge Street parking lot, next to City Hall, honoring Weber Furlong. The marker stated:

Weber Furlong
1878 – 1962
One of America's great and influential artists of the twentieth century, Weber Furlong was among the first to champion the Modern art movement. The final years of her life were spent in Glens Falls, where she lived and taught near this site at her Ridge Street studio until her death in 1962.

Placed for the Warren County Bicentennial

The virtues of the life led by my great-grand-aunt, Wilhelmina Weber, enhanced my life and the lives of those who knew her. This was a life lived independently and was so boldly centered in the artistic cultures of the time. For many years, I have loved and admired the art, and now I am grateful to share the story of my Aunt Wilhelmina. I am the last remaining Weber, like Wilhelmina, I have no children. I hope to encourage artistic pursuits with the creation of this exhibit and the associated Weber Furlong Foundation to preserve her life's work.

This book is dedicated to my father, Bernard Erwin Weber III, who spent time at Golden Heart Farm before and after the accidental death of his father. His insight into the artist was quite evident during his life.

This exhibit and biography carries on her remarkable journey across time. Now she can continue to touch the lives of those who experience the emotion and power of her body of work, her remarkable journey, and appreciate her life experiences and contributions to the history of art in America.

Clint B. Weber

The Weber Furlong Collection of Modern Art

Executive Director and Chief Curator

Miss Wilhelmina Weber at Cuernavaca, Mexico, in 1907.
She is seated in an old churchyard next to a mango tree!

Golden Heart Farm

This story of Wilhelmina Weber Furlong and her husband Thomas "Tomas" Furlong begins at Bolton Landing on Lake George in upstate New York. Wilhelmina lived an astonishing and remarkable life. Throughout her early years, she played roles in some rather interesting historical events. Her life was interwoven and her paths crisscrossed with some commanding figures in world and art history. She became foremost an artist who had the opportunity to experience life outside the United States and then came home to enjoy her life in America. Wilhelmina Weber became part of an emerging class of bold American women who ventured out into the world with uninhibited zeal in the late 1800s. The pioneering nature of her artistic creations in her time is unmistakable when viewed as a whole. She is clearly now defined as a pioneer in the American art community she served. This treasured collection of paintings displays a style that is uniquely hers.

Her life story began at a time in American history when women could begin to express themselves, in the New York schools well before 1900. The Art Students League became the place in America where this would occur. In New York Wilhelmina Weber was highly valued at the Art Students League and drew great respect. Wilhelmina Weber's life was a growth process, to a point of simple understanding, of merging the primitive with the modern, of living in sophistication and in simplicity, a balance between the fine things and the simple things, all understood from the viewpoint of self-expression, self-awareness, and spirituality.

Wilhelmina Weber shared her life with her one true love, her contemporary, Thomas Furlong, also a very talented artist, without whom she was incomplete. They met in a remote region of the world and shared a common interest. They spent time together before they were married, and grew close; she was eight years older than Thomas Furlong was, and in letters to his sister, there was tension between him and his family over this.

He and Wilhelmina Weber were simple, though sophisticated people, who lived from day to day, always in the moment. As a couple, the two never worried about the future and loved each other dearly. They worked hard to save for a retirement in Portugal, a vision the couple would never realize. They created an art colony called Golden Heart, the Weber family farm at Bolton Landing, NY. It was to become a destination of many noted American and international artists, as well as many unknown artists and students of that time who studied and lived at the farm. Many artists were struggling throughout the 1920s, and they always had a place to stay, and good homegrown food to eat, while at Golden Heart. Artists who stayed there gave the Furlongs works of art.

Thomas Furlong and Wilhelmina Weber were dedicated to a life of art and the appreciation of the arts. They were teachers and innovators who helped shape American art during a critical turning point, and the place they held in key circles of the Modern Art movement is remarkable. For them to have been so effectively discussed in public and so well-known even to this very day, the Furlongs played an important role in the history of early American Modern Art. Besides being art teachers to many of the artists in residence at Golden Heart Farm, Thomas Furlong and Wilhelmina Weber were close friends to them all. Thomas was an accomplished concert pianist, who could read and write fluently in English, Spanish, Italian, German, and French.

The Furlongs played a major role at the turn of the century at the Art Students League of New York, where she involved with the Whitney Studio Galleries. After many years of art studies there, Wilhelmina Weber fulfilled the roles as the administrative director of the school, executive board associate, and its treasurer. In 1921, Thomas Furlong became an executive board member of the board of control, and he served as the League's treasurer. From this prestigious venue, Wilhelmina Weber became a well-known figure in the avant-garde movement of the time. During that time, her progressive thought helped to transform the organization into the modern realities present within the art world.

Wilhelmina Weber acquired Golden Heart Farm in 1921 as a summer home. She traveled between her New York studio and Glens Falls from Golden Heart Farm. She would eventually return to Golden Heart and to Bolton Landing. As a single woman, she lived in Greenwich Village, New York, where she painted many of her early works. She was quite popular and rather prolific while in New York City. The couple moved to the summer home permanently in winter of 1939. Wilhelmina Weber moved to Glens Falls as her winter residence in October of 1956, four years after Thomas Furlong passed away. During this time at Golden Heart, she started signing her work "WF," although most of her work went unsigned. Golden Heart became her beloved home cherished above all else, and New York City became her art studio, a place she held close throughout her life. For the duration of her life, she preferred the title Weber. Therefore, many in New York City simply called her Miss Weber.

To begin a chronology, by 1890, at the age of 12, she had already begun to paint and draw while living and studying in St. Louis. Her father quickly recognized her talent. She first passed through the prestigious Art Students League at the age of 14. The year was 1892, and it was the opening season for the Art Students League in Manhattan. It was on a visit from St. Louis to meet William Chase that she was inspired to dedicate herself to becoming an artist and painter. She continued in New York City with Emil Carlsen, and she would eventually begin studying at the St. Louis Academy of Fine Arts between 1894 and

1900. From there, she followed Carlsen and Chase between 1900 and 1903 to the Pennsylvania Academy of Fine Arts in Philadelphia and one year at the school of William Merritt Chase in New York in 1897, where she was a favorite student. At the encouragement of Chase, she would eventually move to Paris to study and paint. In 1898 and 1899, she studied at Washington University in St. Louis under Edmund H. Wuerpel (1866-1958). This would all occur between 1890 and 1902. Another woman student at the Pennsylvania Academy of Fine Arts in Philadelphia thirty-five years earlier was Mary Stevenson Cassatt, 1844-1926.

During the early 1900s, when Wilhelmina was in Paris, she admired the impressionism of Mary Cassatt for a second time, after having seen her exhibit at the 1893 World's Columbian Exposition in Chicago. (The World's Fair pass of Thomas Furlong is in the exhibit's letters.) All of this brilliant exposure led Wilhelmina Weber to the thresholds of America's most prestigious doorways in art. She lived in Paris between 1903 and 1906. She moved to Paris after having spent time there prior to 1900 on trips to draw French boots for her brother Bernard in 1898 and 1899. Among her many friends were Pablo Picasso, Gertrude Stein, and Paul Cézanne. By 1903 at the age of 22, she was well on her way to becoming one of the institution's first woman activists, and she became an artist of established reputation before her marriage in 1921. Her wealthy father, without objection from her mother, funded the young Miss Wilhelmina Weber's travels as; she had their full support to pursue a carefree life of painting. At the Salons of Gertrude Stein in Paris, she would meet and be influenced by Henri Matisse between 1905 and 1906.

By 1914, she had begun to teach painting to those who passed through the grand gallery hall of the Art Students League in Manhattan, and she had become an established administrator before her departure. Many years later, she would study with Max Weber in 1920, after her return to

New York in 1913 from Mexico City. She became a close friend of John Graham's in 1920, shortly after his arrival in the United States. In New York, before her marriage, Wilhelmina Weber devoted her life to art and to the Art Students League. After she married Thomas Furlong, their studio at #122 East 59th Street became the Furlong Studio. The two occupied this location from 1913 to 1924.

The Glens Falls Times in 1966 described her as a pioneer of the Modern Art Movement; Wilhelmina Weber Furlong became deeply entrenched in the lives of some of America's greatest modern painters, who were friends and companions. Known for her outspoken views and lively comments to her family and friends, she travelled throughout France, while studying in Paris, and she also lived in and painted the countryside outside of Mexico City before her marriage to Thomas Furlong. Weber provided private lessons and served as a tutor to numerous artists and students of the period. For a brief time, artists such as Donald Judd, Georgia O'Keeffe, and others would pass through the Art Students League's halls during her time in New York.

Her influence on Modern Art remains. As we explore her life, we will come to understand what produced this international woman, and how she helped to shape others through her art and her intercontinental experiences. This was an exciting time in American art history, and artists such as Weber had a profound influence on the movement.

During the decades after her life, she would be hailed as distinguished artist and beloved teacher, and memorialized by a community that has never lost its love of her life, remembered by her many friends and associates. Weber's lifelong credo will not be forgotten.

"To live is to paint," Weber Furlong

Reflecting back to the early days of Wilhelmina Weber's youth, much is left to the imagination. We do know that she had some of the most accomplished mentors and teachers available before the turn of the 20th century. She started painting as an adolescent in 1890 with the close attention and support of her father and brother. While in Mexico, she was exploring the Latin American cultures, a region of the world she would come to know and love.

We know that, on more than a few occasions, between 1898 and 1906 she spent a great deal of time in several Paris salons. Paris was of great significance to her, and she became deeply impacted by the people she met. She would meet many of the significant artists within the private salons that had formed after 1889. This would expose her to Picasso, whom she knew quite well, and Matisse, as well as figures from the literary world. She spoke often about Gertrude Stein (1874-1946) and her life in Paris. Items she collected there are included in the Weber Furlong Collection.

We know Wilhelmina Weber painted while in Paris, and the collection includes examples of her earliest work between 1892 and 1906. Her Parisian Canvases are the most stunning of the collection. It was at this time she would use watercolor as a means of expression. The influence of Henri Matisse (1869–1954) and Paul Cézanne (1839-1906) is quite evident in the watercolors on display. They are classic and true to form. This detail surely indicates instruction from the master Matisse in his style and Cézanne in his. Painted in Paris between 1898 and 1906, they are brightly colored and clearly still life watercolor at its very best. For the most part, she quit painting watercolor after departing Paris and moved to oil on canvas.

Wilhelmina Weber spent her entire life painting and experimenting with her work, as a teenage girl, by 1890 and as a fully developed artist in New York, where she clearly influenced some of the great American modernists within her community. The Young Wilhelmina Weber was fluent in French, therefore her life in Paris was much easier, and for an extended period, she was quite comfortable. She had been encouraged at a young age by Emil Carlsen to experience both the city and country life surrounding Paris. She was one of his favorite students, and he felt this would be important to her. Her father Bernard and mother Maggie supported this as an important undertaking for her art studies. Her brother with his French boot making ventures in St Louis also encouraged and assisted with her studies in Paris, France where she initially illustrated for the family business.

Salon in Paris, France, ca. 1898-1906

Wilhelmina Weber did not always travel alone. Her cousin Wilhelmina (Mina) Meyer accompanied her on some of her travels. While studying in the Paris salons, the two experienced their happiest days together. The previous photo shows Mina Meyer seated on the canapé-lit. Wilhelmina Weber is serenading her. Music was of great interest to her cousin Mina.

The two stayed in Mexico during the initial visit in 1906, and they stayed together off and on for several years during their more youthful days. They traveled to many places and stayed in very comfortable apartments. Their wealthy fathers, who loved them dearly, supported all their endeavors up to adulthood and marriage. The topic of family conversation was their travels together. They seem to have lived carefree lives of adventure and opportunity for young women of the day.

From viewing many of Wilhelmina Weber's travel photos, it is safe to say that she loved flowers, seeing her surrounded by them outside and in vegetable gardens is a common occurrence. One of the collection's highlights is the exhibition photo of the young woman at work in Paris, painting outside at her best, and looking quite content at work. It has become the artist's headline poster and a trademark image of Wilhelmina Weber. She was painting before the turn of the century, as a young woman who, shaped by her great mentors, had a profound love of art. This is the great artist living her life's passion; a passion which developed as a child in St. Louis and lasted throughout her lifetime. Because of this devout passion, she was educated and highly trained at a time when women would come to great institutions and to great masters to be skilled at their doorsteps in growing numbers.

She shared many of the encounters about her life in Paris with her students, who immediately noticed the mannerisms associated with her unique experiences in France.

In the photographs below, we see comparison photos of a teenage Wilhelmina Weber in St Louis and the adult artist in one of her two great homes in Mexico City. Her first home was near the San Juan de Letran train station, and her second was a large home near el hospital Real, in Mexico City. Two places in the city that we know she lived, while in Mexico. She lived in Xochimilco before moving to Mexico City however, we do not know the address of this hacienda or the exact location. We do know she was with a wealthy landowner and quite possibly the family of Felix Diaz. She did know General Diaz and his family. They were well acquainted and looked after her throughout her stay in Mexico.

Mexico City   St. Louis

Remote Xochimilco Canals, south of the central city 1908

In Mexico City, she was acquainted with Carmen Romero Rubio, the wife of President Porfirio Diaz, and they shared their love of Mexico. The two were well acquainted, and it was common to see the first lady at public or social events. During her local travels with the first lady of Mexico, armed family members and men accompanied them for protection. One of them, Felix Diaz, would eventually plot to overthrow the Mexican government during the Madero revolution. She was clearly fortunate to have left Mexico when she did.

Wilhelmina loved Mexico City, and she spent a great deal of time traveling in Central and South America during her lengthy stay. She loved the native art and colorful dress of the native women she encountered and she enjoyed shopping for local art and antiques.

Remote Xochimilco Canals, south of the central city, 1908

The Golden Heart Collection includes numerous photographs of her travels throughout the region. As my father told me, her time there was of special significance to her. She took excursions to remote regions, and boated down the rivers and lakes in isolated and dangerous areas of Latin America. Wilhelmina Weber was indeed a very strong-willed woman, well ahead of her time. She undoubtedly was quite the adventurous and spirited woman who also loved the Central American and Guatemalan cultures. Her travels took her too many of the familiar places and ruins we still see today; however, in those days, getting there was not an easy task. The Aztec and Mayan shards she picked up in her travels throughout southern Mexico are part of the treasures exhibited in the collection.

A number of her experiences and stories were verbal and came to me from my father and mother. However, most came from reading her letters and notes. From this family research, we know Mexico was of great romance to her, a place she enjoyed at the turn of the century. Arriving in

Mexico City in 1906, intending to stay only two weeks, she spent time visiting the Presidential bastion, resulting in travel guides provided for her by the President of Mexico. She would stay seven years. We know she lived in numerous places throughout Mexico during her tenure there.

Fortunately, with her fluency in English, French, German, and Spanish, Wilhelmina Weber made herself available as an interpreter to the President of Mexico, through his nephew Felix Diaz. As an interpreter, she would have been among his most trusted inner circle. She would have been well cared for, while in service to the first family of Mexico. It was in this capacity she met her future husband, Thomas "Tomas" Furlong, who was there translating for his father in confidential affairs with President Diaz concerning Furlong Secret Service Agency business matters. Thomas Furlong's father was a famous Civil War veteran, and founder of the Thomas Furlong Secret Service Company of St. Louis, Houston, and Cincinnati.

Weber also grew elaborate flower gardens while staying in Mexico. Flower and vegetable gardening were among her many favorite pastimes. The young adventure-minded Wilhelmina Weber would visit the canals of Xochimilco long before they had begun to dry up from water usage, and the expansion of Mexico City. Today, only remnants remain of this vast pre-Spanish colonial conquest network of rivers and waterways, a part of ancient Mexico forever lost. At that time, the canal system would have been much more remote and quite a bit more extensive, than as seen today.

She collected many things while in Mexico and we have a good record of her travels there. Hers was a working professional-life, one in which she was well compensated for her service.

Wilhelmina's seven years in Mexico City was a long time to spend 2,600 miles from home, as a young single woman in the early 1900s. In her later years, she talked about Latin America often. She survived there on her own merits and abilities. Strong-willed and capable of achieving much ready and able to strike out on her own to make a lasting difference to society, Wilhelmina Weber was such a woman both in her life and in her art, and she profoundly affected those she met throughout the years, into the present.

Artifacts found by Wilhelmina Weber, 1906-1913

Wilhelmina Weber was a part of an élite circle in Mexico, a teacher of French and English to several of her friends and language to the children of wealthy Mexican politicians I am sure she came to know and love many of them. Subsequently, some of her favorite times were spent in the beautiful mysterious places behind the walls of great palatial homes and haciendas. The gardens and courtyards of Mexico are renowned for their beauty, and a place for festive celebrations. It was a well-respected way of life for that time in Mexico. She would talk about the magnificent stables and horses she would come to see and experience while working in Mexico. Often on horseback, while her close friends observed and made note of it, she would ride across the countryside at near full gallop better than some men would even attempt.

She traveled extensively, and lived in comfort for many years. The family never sent her large sums of money, and from what we know, she never sold many paintings while there. Had it not been for the Mexican revolution, it might have never ended for her. Her education afforded her the opportunity to make a respected living, while her art instruction gave her inner peace and a close awareness of who she really was.

Given the number of notes and photographs in the collection, her years in Mexico were some of her fondest memories. Wilhelmina Weber lived in a very large, well-furnished apartment with a grand sitting room on Callejon Espiritu, in Cuernavaca. Between 1906 and 1913, among her closest friends was Mrs. B. C. Hill, who lived at Apartado 233 Cuernavaca Morelos, Mexico. The two spent time together and shared a lifelong friendship. They are in several of the photographs in the Archives. Mrs. Hill sent nostalgic photographs to Wilhelmina in 1960, to update her on the current state of her favorite places in southern Mexico. They had taken numerous picnics at Xochimilco. Cuernavaca was a political hot seat for President Diaz by 1910. The movement to oust his government, which had started there, had evolved into armed bandits and anti-Diaz factions. Political change was in the air for President Diaz, and Emilio Zapata became a local leader to the south of Mexico City midyear in 1909.

Wilhelmina in the Callejon Espiritu sitting room, ca. 1912

Driven from her home nine miles south of Mexico City in Xochimilco because life became much too dangerous for Americans, she became part of the upheaval as one living through the ordeal. There was strong anti-American sentiment during all three uprisings of the revolution. She fled her home during the early battles of the revolution, and she often spoke of the smell of gunpowder and the sounds of gunfire cracking in the distant hills outside her quarters. She took an apartment at San Juan de Letran in Mexico City. Like most Mexican women, she lived fearless of the troubles that surrounded them daily.

The Sunday edition of the New York Tribune on May 10, 1914 highlighted women of the day in two kinds of revolutions: The revolt of young working women against the established authority in labor strife, and Wilhelmina Weber's artistic experience during the Mexican Revolution. In the article, she portrayed the beautiful women of Mexico and their culture caught up in political strife, and the destruction of vast collections of historic treasures held by the aristocracy that were sold off on the streets for mere pennies.

In Mexico, she experienced the transition of the local art forms, as she described it, into a much less traditional "souvenir-hunter" version of the centuries-old Spanish style. Sophisticated colors, bright dyes, and Mexican clay resembling Spain's Talavera tiles caught her artistic eye. Soft yellows, greens, old blues, and vermilion are words she used to describe local art and architecture throughout Mexico.

San Juan de Letran, Mexico, 1910

Collection photos reveal Wilhelmina Weber played the piano, as a child in St Louis and as a young woman in Mexico. The San Juan de Letran apartment in Mexico City had a Victorian grand piano seen in the photo above. She is said to have played quite well and was able to teach her music skills to her students while in Mexico. This represents less troublesome day's safe inside Mexico City after her hasty full late night flight from Xochimilco during the height of the Mexican insurrection.

Southern Mexico and the Primitive Experience

At this point in her travels, we will examine some of her Mexico paintings and her accounts, complete with a secret garden in Cuernavaca! First, is the Primitive Mayan Indian woman relaxing by the river; this is an early work from her days in Mexico. This significant painting attests to the feelings for a culture she held close to her throughout her life. On the back of it, hidden from view, is a drawing of complete and sheer astonishment. It appears to be a man in his night-clothes, reading a book by a window. Is it a romance? Why is it on the back of a painting? The long nose and eyebrows add detail, and his mustache appears hidden with an apple. Was this a powerful general or politician? The subject could not be the man she would eventually marry. At the time of its creation, she had not met Thomas Furlong so we might assume it is a close and cherished friend maybe even a secret or private romance.

We may never know the man's identity, but could this be the reason the two-week excursion lasted seven years? The Mexican Revolution unmistakably disrupted her life, the logical result of changing political times. Was the man in the painting someone she had hopelessly loved under difficult circumstances? It clearly must have been someone of special significance to her. This is an intimate moment captured on the artist's canvas, preserved for us to speculate about. What a most interesting conjecture this painting adds to a life she had come to adore and express through her painting. Even more powerful is a stunning image of someone long since forgotten to time and to the ravages of a civil war far from her home back in America. This war-torn devastation in Mexico was something she had come to know quite well and in that uncertainty, she found time for romance and for moments that were more tranquil such as this.

The secret image, Mexico, ca. 1906-1910

The Primitive Mayan Indian woman, relaxing by a river in southern Mexico, ca. 1906-1910

After examining the literature and reading the personal letters in Wilhelmina's estate, we can presume that the culture that had led her to such a close bond with the Hills was the Indian cultures of the Yucatan peninsula. This was significant to her life in Cuernavaca and it was during this time, 1906-1910, that Wilhelmina Weber would paint the Mayan woman. This work of art, which she created before meeting Thomas Furlong, tells a story of social understanding and her cultural compassion.

Further scrutiny reveals that Mr. and Mrs. Hill were close friends of the noted author Stuart Chase, said to have coined the term "New Deal." After their dearest friend Wilhelmina Weber returned to New York, the couple assisted Chase with his travels across Mexico, while doing research for his book *A Study of Two Americas*. Mrs. Hill sent Wilhelmina Weber a copy of Chase's book after its publication in 1931, also seen in the exhibit of her belongings.

The predicament of the Indian cultures was of great concern to Wilhelmina Weber. Along with the difficulties they would encounter, she became influenced by their traditions and their unique society. Their civilization had seen great losses and the life they had at that time was a very difficult one. Additionally, the agricultural difficulties of their region and the country overall were of concern. She experienced the poverty, the struggle of remote villages firsthand and clearly identified with these people and with their troubled history. She admired their handcraft creativity, and she above all loved the colorful pottery and brilliant colored fabrics. Her Latin American travels clearly influenced her life and helped to shape the woman who would bring her skills to New York's Greenwich Village at the Art Students League and at Golden Heart Farm for so many years.

Mexico, 1906-1912

Cuernavaca at the Hotel Buenavista, 1909-1910

After meeting Thomas Furlong in 1912, the couple spent a little more than a year together in Old Mexico. Wilhelmina Weber even earned the nickname "Webercita" from her close friends in America. She visited the old church at Acapantzingo, and often stayed in Cuernavaca at the Hotel Buenavista. She would spend some time contemplating on the rooftop in 1909. A friend writes on the snapshot, "Weber, here you are contemplating Cuernavaca from the roof top of the hotel – I forgot its name, Buenavista? That must have been about 1909. Yesterday, June 20, 1947, I went into the half-ruinous patio of the same building – the same heavy low arches, and some good balconies still exist. The old place could be restored, if anyone were interested. It is about the only building in that state which remains."

Reading her books, studying her life, and understanding her close contacts have revealed the diverse and remarkable life of Wilhelmina Weber. It has helped to release the woman from an elapsed history and experience her from a more modern perspective with clarity and understanding. We can appreciate her influence by stepping back to a time when people worked hard to help foster a greater understanding of the struggles within a culture. Back to a time when people worked hard to influence the world by making this struggle known through their artistic and literary creations. America and Mexico at that time had been through difficult social and transitional times as the world progressed to a more modern society. Many artists and scholars would embrace this change. Even today, that same struggle continues as we deal with the harsh realities of our time. When future generations look back, will we be considered in the same light? Will our art show and reflect the realities of our time? Surly the artistic and creative mark our society leaves behind will charm those who desire to understand us.

The Garden in Casa Blanca, San Ángel, México City 1906

MEXICO is the last place one would look for art in these troubled days, and especially Futurist art, yet it is from Mexico that Miss Wilhelmine Weber got her inspiration for the glowing painted furniture which has taken New York captive as the latest fad in interior decoration. As for that, even into exterior decoration has modernism extended, for Miss Weber and her co-worker, Thomas Furlong, are now decorating a garden in a country estate with Slavic-blue fences striped benches.

Miss Weber has been in New York but one year, and already has her distinctive niche among artists, yet she sighs at the plight of the country from which she absorbed the lessons which made it possible for her to make her art individual with sun-drenched beauty.

Into the technique of a formal art education Miss Weber brought the spirit of Mexico, with its sunshine and dazzling colors, which she absorbed in the years she "vagabondaged" there. So that when she speaks of Mexico it is with understanding of the crude yet vibrant spirit of the Spanish-Indian race.

Mexico Riots with Happiness.

She becomes very enthusiastic when she speaks of Mexico. "It is the most wonderful beautiful place," Miss Weber says. "I always think of it as a land rioting with happiness, not as one devastated by bandits and black with smoking ruins. This, too, in spite of the fact that I lived through three revolutions, nine miles from the City of Mexico, and that we were finally driven from our home by the noise of battle just over the hill.

"We expected at any moment that the fight would spread into our town, and we feared we could not trust to the kind feeling of our neighbors to overcome the anti-American prejudices of their countrymen. At all events, a town clamoring with battle is no place to woo the muse and we felt it timely to depart.

"Mexico is radiant with wonderful lemon white sunshine that glorifies everything and brings out the beauty of all the dazzling colors the people love. Americans who are not well informed think Mexico is made up of terra cotta and mud color. Nothing is more false. The people revel in brilliant colors. They use red and purple dyes even on their floors. After the floor has been scrubbed to a dazzling cleanliness they take a pail full of dye and splash it on, swishing it around with a broom.

"If a woman gets tired of her white muslin dress she dips it in the dyeing pail. Imagine the color effect of a woman in an orange skirt in a room with a lemon yellow floor, with furni-ture of a deep purple, lighted by touches of red!

Mexicans Love Brilliant Colors.

"The Mexicans are not afraid of color, you see. They dare all these wonderful effects which Americans have not the courage to adopt. We cling to dismal old gray-greens and blues, and, of course, we get despondent and think the world is full of trouble. The Mexican puts on her red skirt and her green shawl and laughs at trouble."

When Miss Weber made her first visit to Mexico she found the country rich with art treasures completely overlooked by the eager collectors who ransack everything from a New England farmhouse to an Italian peasant's hovel. She brought back to the United States precious antiques, and called the attention of the connoisseurs and travellers to be had for objects and furniture to be had for almost nothing in the pawnshops.

Their Art Is Not Crude.

"All the art of Mexico is not the crude art of the peons, however. The old towns are full of exquisite bits of Talavera pottery, such as are treasured to-day in the British Museum. This is the art of the Spanish invaders. When Cortez and his followers settled Mexico they brought over with them Talavera tiles.

"They soon discovered that there was a kind of clay in the north of Mexico which was very similar to the Talavera clay, so they began the manufacturing of tiles on a large scale. The domes of the old churches to-day are covered with these wonderful tiles in soft yellows, greens, old blues and vermilion. The jars in the apothecary shops and the household pottery are made of this same wonderful tiling.

"Then, too, the Spanish conquerors brought over boatloads of the most beautiful art treasures that Europe knew at that time. They were aristocrats, you know. They brought rich tapestries for their churches and beautiful furniture for their palaces. Much of this is now to be picked up in the pawnshops, since the old families have died out or have had their taste perverted by a certain American standard which can only understand the price of things, not their artistic value.

"The revolution, of course, has meant the undoing of many of the old family fortunes, too, and priceless tapestries which have hung on palace walls for centuries are now to be picked up by the tactful collector for a song.

American Tourists Destroy Standards.

"It is quite true that the modern art of Mexico is being destroyed by the American tourist. The beautiful old vases and jars which the peons have made for centuries according to the standards set by their Spanish masters in the old days are now being altered to suit the souvenir hunter.

"Perhaps some American thought it would be nice to have a Mexican flag set on the side of the jar, so he could remember where he bought it, I suppose. The peon, eager to please the dispenser of gold, drew a flag in the jar, which was quite out of harmony with the pure color of the pottery. Then along came other souvenir hunters who thought it would be even better to have two flags, the American and the Mexican, crossed. To do this meant that the potter must broaden his vase, and thus the destruction of the perfect form was accomplished.

"Please do not imagine that the Futurist furniture which we are making now is a product of the Mexican art. The Mexican is a decadent art. Our furniture has been influenced by the crude Slavic art of Bohemia and South Germany. Mexico's part in my career is that while there I learned to love bright colors, and when I returned to this country, after five years there, I was ready to learn the lessons of Europe as I could not have done had I not had preliminary training in Mexico.

Decadence Wedded to Innocence.

"The South of Germany and the little known country north and east of Vienna is where one must go to-day to find real color in innocent abandon. The people there use it even on their fences, and the little kiosks, which are like Swiss chalets, are covered with conventional flowers and birds in all sorts and colors.

Miss Weber and her partner, Thomas Furlong, are having a lovely time making a blue, green and white garden set for a wealthy Long Island landholder. The fence is to be of alternate green and white pickets, with the thickness of the boards painted black. The summer house and gateways are to have broad bands of blue.

"I don't know why people think their garden benches must be green always," said Miss Weber, in explaining this creation. "Every color is beautiful in the bright sunlight with a background of green. A bit of color in the landscape makes the most perfect garden a brighter and pleasanter place."

Sunday, May 14, 1914 New York Tribune

33

At that time, (1906-1929) before the Great Depression, the Weber family was still quite wealthy. Her father's holdings included land and several real estate ventures. His primary business was the wholesale supply of candy and dry goods from the port city of St. Louis to places unknown, and eventually to San Antonio, Texas, where her brother, Bernard, would become a shoe and boot proprietor, after moving his business to Texas from St. Louis. As a confectioner, August C. Weber was successful, and Texas brought more diversity to the family business.

After getting financial assistance from his father, the young Bernard Weber became a very successful French boot manufacturer. His shop originally in St. Louis, was moved to San Antonio, where he supplied the Guarantee Shoe Store and other department stores in San Antonio. The expansion of the business ventures to San Antonio was a big step for the Weber family. Bernard's business remained successful for many years, until the death of his son Bernard Weber II, after an automobile accident in 1942. While returning to San Antonio from a business trip, his car veered off the road into a railroad crossing over the highway and he was fatally injured. In his later years, he became the Secretary-Treasurer of the South Western Shoe Travelers Association. He traveled to France on occasion, accompanied by his sister Wilhelmina Weber and their younger cousin Mina Meyer.

Early in her life, the young Miss Wilhelmina Weber was by no means fully independent. She had financial support and her brother Bernard supervised her, at her father's request, on occasions when he was away tending to important business. Throughout his life Wilhelmina Weber's father displayed endearment to the artist in the family. Bernard Weber would write his sister Wilhelmina Weber all through his life. There was a real sense of sadness in the days they were apart, and since the death of his son Bernard E. Weber II, the attachment to my father was even stronger. This loss led young Ben (Bernard E Weber III) to the farm in Bolton Landing. The tragic accident would bring him to Golden Heart for more than just his summers. At the time of the accident, he was fourteen. By the mid 1930s, he had been spending time at the farm from the age of seven. His mother, Jean Johnston Weber, my grandmother, never really got over the loss of her husband Bernard Weber II.

During the Civil War, some of the Weber family's southern farm products and food supplies of the family business had been conscripted by the Confederacy, surely to the family's dismay. (The Civil War conscription document is in the exhibit archives.) The Collection includes numerous Civil War memorabilia, even an old slightly damaged sword from the St. Louis riot at Camp Jackson in 1861. The German population of St Louis was quite loyal to the Union during that time, and formed a large volunteer regiment. The port city of St. Louis was one of the most active and important cities during the war, so the Union maintained a strong presence, allowing the Weber and Meyer families to prosper. Some of the family on her father's side had moved to San Antonio, so the family, like many others, became separated during the Civil War. Wilhelmina Weber's cousin, Wilhelmina (Mina) Meyer tells the story in family letters, as follows:

"Wilhelmina Weber's mother Magdelina (Maggie) Meyer was born in 1846 in Lexington, Missouri. Her father Francis came from Rothweil-Baden, Germany in 1848, during the freedom movement in Germany. They fled Germany during the rebellion against the tyranny of barons, and in search of economic freedom."

This is the story as told by Wilhelmina Weber, as she had heard it from her mother Maggie:

"There were three Meyer bothers in total that had sailed from Germany: Joe, Bernhard, and Francis. They had sailed from Havre, France taking 54 days to reach New Orléans. Each passenger had to carry his own food - it must have been a miserable experience. Wilhelmina Weber's uncle Bernhardt Meyer had been appointed as a monitor to keep the young people in order. They then traveled up the Mississippi river to St Louis, and Francis traveled up the Missouri River eventually to Lexington, Kentucky. Bernhard and his brother Joe started a grocery store. Shortly after arriving Joe was dissatisfied and took off for parts unknown. Long afterwards, the family received news from Germany that he and his wife had died in Germany."

The grocery store and bakery continued into modern times as "Baker Meyer's". Wilhelmina (Minnie) Weber, the artist, and her cousin Wilhelmina (Mina) Meyer would visit them often, sitting primly on old horsehair parlor chairs, sipping homemade wine from dainty stemmed glasses. Minnie and Mina were very close friends, and it was Wilhelmina Weber who would keep the family history alive, during the hours spent reminiscing with her cousin Mina.

Bernhardt Meyer's prosperous wholesale grocery business afforded them a house near the river wharf, where all commercial traffic came by steamboat. In her personal letters, we learn that there were numerous stories about her family's Civil War days. Like many, they had endured numerous hardships and Wilhelmina (Mina) Meyer said there were strong family ties to keep them together during this difficult and emotional time.

I want to bring both family histories to the forefront, because on their death, the ashes of her father, August C. Weber, Magdelina (Maggie) Meyer, her mother, and Thomas Furlong, her husband, were scattered at Golden Heart Farm. Eventually Wilhelmina Weber's ashes were scattered there as well; two generations of family on the mountaintop retreat.

Wilhelmina Weber's days at Golden Heart Farm

The landscapes painted at Golden Heart reveal the deep bond she felt for the Lake George countryside and the small community of Bolton Landing, New York. Several of these paintings are among the earliest examples of modern German expressionism in the style of the Fauves created in America. They are also diverse and largely varied in form and style. Some depict life at Golden Heart while others are abstract and display vivid colors. Some even depict still-life tables brought out into the Lake George countryside. These are a result of using the bright sunlight to capture an object's essence and color to understand how objects change in varying settings.

"The Little Houses" at Golden Heart Farm, as she called them, were five minutes from the Bolton Landing ferry, and she wrote about them as being quaint and relaxing to vacation in from the big city. There were five of them in total and one of them colorfully depicted in an eye-catching blue and windy watercolor captivates many. There are numerous photographs of these cabins, which symbolize the art colonies lasting influence on the community.

Wilhelmina (Mina) Meyer preserved the family history by writing most of the information down as remembered by Wilhelmina Weber and her mother. This was because Mina was the last of the Meyer family.

One of several "Little House" studios at Golden Heart Farm

During the early 1930's Wilhelmina Weber's Cousin Wilhelmina (Mina) Meyer, who had remained in Lexington, Missouri, eventually purchased a cabin next to Golden Heart Farm from the Furlongs. The cabin was small and had served as one of the artist Little Houses and it was on the opposite side of the county road at the entrance to Golden Heart Farm. Mina traveled often to her quaint little cabin, which had no indoor plumbing. Mina became a summer resident and remained part of the Bolton Landing community for many years. Mina Meyer remained very close to Wilhelmina Weber throughout her life.

In her later years before her death, Mina would drive from Lexington to Bolton Landing in an old Volkswagen beetle that had seen its better days. George Barber recalls it was amazing the old VW beetle even made the trip. Mina also traveled with her brother, Frank E. Meyer who also lived in Lexington. Frank like Mina had no children.

Wilhelmina Weber's brother, Bernard Weber knew what Thomas Furlong and his sister had at Golden Heart Farm and he knew how much she loved it there. Throughout the Second World War, the two communicated about family life, and there was regular mention of General John Perry Willey (1902-1976), the Brigadier General who married Mary Elizabeth Weber, Bernard's daughter and was the Commanding General of the 5332nd Brigade (Mars Brigade) Burma in 1945.

Artists who stayed with the Furlongs at Golden Heart included David Smith, John Graham, Stuart Chase, Dorothy Dehner, Jean Charolot, Alexander Calder, Rockwell and Sally Kent, Thomas Hart Benton, Allen Tucker, Max Weber, and Kimon Nicolaidies. Many of these artists were very close to Thomas Furlong and Wilhelmina Weber. Many of them also spent time contemplating in the Little Houses of the art colony. They even traveled together with several of them. Each Little House had a unique name, however we only know the name of one, called Saint Swithin's Tool House.

Life for her at Golden Heart became much more difficult as she began to feel the effects of old age. Harsh New York winters, no indoor plumbing, and a long hike up a steep hill to fetch water, vegetable gardening for food to eat, and wood gathering to cook and stay warm complicated her life. She had no running hot water and no springhouse or well to simplify things. In her final declining years, she had a long rope tied around her waist as blindness set in, that she used to drag two large ceramic brown and white water jugs up from the creek. The rope looped through the finger holes in the jugs, a second rope led her to the spring at the creek. However, during her golden years, life for her throughout the 1950s was no different from life in the 1890s countryside surrounding Bolton Landing. She had to get by with very little in terms of our modern way of life. She was not destitute. She simply held on to her simple lifestyle until it became impossible to maintain in her old age. She had friends and students who brought her things and helped her prepare for the winter. Weber had a golden heart, she lived her life for other people, and she even gave up her career for her husband Thomas Furlong. Bolton Landing, is to this very day, a very friendly community and many local families loved her. Throughout the years, the community she touched understood her hardships. She and Dorothy Dehner remained friends. A young George Barber of Bolton helped with the difficult tasks she needed and for that, he inherited half of her remaining land in her last Will and Testament. He eventually purchased the second half from the estate in 1987. George Barber was a much-loved student of Thomas and Weber Furlongs. He and his daughter Eileen were with Wilhelmina Weber in 1962 shortly before she passed away. George would open Golden Heart Farm for Wilhelmina Weber during the last ten years of her life. He describes the barns as being set up with all the still-life tables and objects for her students to paint. He would also clean the spring for her return from Glens Falls in the springtime - Weber's favorite time of the year. He and his wife Betty would stay in the Little House close to the main house behind the barns whenever they came to assist their dear friend.

Eileen recalls the artist was blind, confined to bed, and not able to see her. The George Barber family was endeared to the elderly woman they had come to know and love. The bond grew after the sudden and unexpected death of Thomas Furlong in 1952 of a heart attack while on campus at Champlain College. George assisted with the difficult adjustment of the loss of Weber's beloved Thomas. Several days later, he was with Wilhelmina Weber at Physicians Hospital when Professor Thomas Furlong passed away.

Eileen B. Allen in her own words recalls: "The close friendship with both Thomas and Weber changed my dad's vision of the world around him. Dad was Thomas' student at Champlain College in Plattsburgh, NY. Growing up, dad would say that Weber and Thomas taught him that every time you see something, it has changed whether you notice it or not. It affected all of my brothers and sisters and made us appreciate the landscapes around us even more. I remember visiting Weber in the early 1960's, she was in a Little House in Glens Falls, the sun was pouring in the room, it must have been shortly before she passed away, she was bedridden I was about 6 years-old. Of course she could not see, but she was eager to meet me and touched my face to 'see' what I looked like."

Wilhelmina Weber would always invite close family like my mom and dad to the farm to experience the relaxed way of life. During her final years, she described the "Little Houses" as neglected, and in a serious state of decline, with the exception of the small studio gallery house pictured in the photograph below. She did think people might still camp out in them in 1960 and still have a great time, if one was so inclined. She treasured the Little Houses. To her, they were a place to re-focus on life's important, yet simple things. They surely represent an important time in American art history, given the many well-known figures that enjoyed their charm.

The second Little House studio with a view of the first Little House, ca. 1921

Sales receipts from Golden Heart Farm reveal that Wilhelmina's hard-working daily life included the purchase of cows, chickens, and pigs. They would raise them, care for them, and eat them whenever necessary. Wilhelmina would kill, clean, and prepare the meal for all their guests. There were no hired hands or servants to assist her. They grew a complete and rather large vegetable crop, tended the garden, and traded the fruits of the harvest locally. The very large garden was directly in a pasture in front of the farmhouse, which had a magnificent view of Lake George. Any spare time meant the family would gather in the front yard under the large trees, weather permitting.

Shoulder height rock walls surrounded the pastures around Golden Heart Farm. They were quite impressive and looked tall. They were composed of huge over-sized boulders interlocked, two rows thick. Outdoor cisterns and small in-ground rock-lined tanks captured rainwater for the garden and livestock when needed. These had a dual purpose; to cool things down for a refreshing drink. There was no well: therefore, water buckets were quite prevalent. The kitchen sink had no water and there was no indoor plumbing. Wilhelmina Weber drew water at the nearby stream in beautiful pitchers. My mother told me that many of them became scratched, chipped, and broken in the process. Water heated by fire in huge pots on top of the wood-burning heaters in the winter served its purpose. The large farmhouse heated by fireplace and wood-burning stoves, with water tanks on the side of several of them, was where the couple shared their moments with visiting students and teachers. Every visitor was welcome and made to feel at home.

The washrooms had metal bathtubs, and some of them were ornate. However, most of them were not. She washed clothing in large metal washtubs, and then she hung it out to dry. Each room had antique washbasins with matching pitchers, of which only one survived. The old farmhouse, illuminated with beautiful crystal and glass oil lamps and lanterns, was welcoming. Thomas Furlong had a grand piano, and he entertained their guests with his concert skills in the large living room at Golden Heart. The Little Houses scattered about the hillside had smaller, more basic oil lamps and wood-burning stoves heated them. Only one of the Little Houses had a small makeshift kitchen that she had painted blue and orange. The Little Houses were for artists in residence. The great barns built of traditional hand-hewn Adirondack timbers became immense art studios where artists and students painted indoors and out. They maintained a stretching bench with tools to prepare their canvas for painting cost effectively.

The massive barns at Golden Heart, 1921

Today only one large barn remains. The others have fallen victim to age. They are lost to time.

"Saint Swithin's Tool House" directly behind the farmhouse, ca. 1921

Wilhelmina Weber's Golden Heart Farm Water Basin

Golden Heart Creek 1921

   Pictured here is the creek near Golden Heart, used from 1921 to 1956 by the artist for collecting water for cooking, bathing, and drinking all year round. By 1960, no longer able to spend her summers at Golden Heart, she would eventually list it for sale; she was 82 years-old, and had lived with no electricity or indoor plumbing at Golden Heart Farm the entire time. Within a year, her death would come in her studio in Glens Falls, at the age of 83. (One could imagine with paintbrush or pen in hand). Wilhelmina Weber Furlong, born November 11, 1878, died May 25, 1962.

Title "Winter" Lake George landscape Golden Heart Farm
1924

The couple had two dogs during their time together, Patricia I and Patricia II. Registration records described both dogs as a blend of briar croft and tan Airedale Terriers, the latter acquired in 1923, both licensed in the City of New York and Bolton Landing. There are photos of the couple with the family dog in the exhibit.

Their life at Golden Heart became a desirable way of life, outside the metropolitan norm and many artists came to see it as one they too, needed. Among them would be painters, sculptors, photographers, and writers. Many of them would become celebrated individuals, like Rockwell Kent, Kenneth Hayes Miller, David Smith, Dorothy Dehner, and John Graham. Never forgotten are the many teachers from the Art Students League who visited Golden Heart and Weber in her quaint big house gallery.

At that time, a rural setting filled with discussions among artists was considered to be improving to one's work, an environment conducive to enhancement. The retreat or colony concept in 1900 was relatively new. Golden Heart was among the first to initiate the practice, in such a back-to-basics setting, generally refusing some modern luxuries. It was a well-thought-out plan by Wilhelmina Weber, and she left New York every summer to put the plan in action. This woman knew what she needed to make the concept work. It was her passion, and a passion shared by her husband.

Some of these reasons could have led to the couple's popularity. They practiced a "free from distractions" style of living. The two painted as modernists. They were among the first in the movement. They were comfortable and creative. With their sophistication understood, many artists came to respect them for their enriched lifestyle. They had led numerous persons to the road that led to Bolton Landing and to the retreat. Countless art lovers came to know and love the community through Golden Heart. This significant undertaking began in the spring of 1921 and lasted until the winter of 1960 by then her health had declined to a point that this free spirit lifestyle could not be maintained due to her age and failing eyesight.

The rather large sum of money to begin the endeavor and acquire the farm came from Wilhelmina Weber's brother, Bernard Weber. Though an example of how much her prosperous brother loved and supported her idea, it did not please his wife Maggie Mae Knapp. Maggie Mae was my great-grandmother, and she lived with her husband in the

Menger Hotel in San Antonio Texas, from 1931 to 1965, where I remember visiting her many times as a small child. At the turn of the 20th century, she made her living selling horses a few blocks from the Alamo.

Wilhelmina's brother, Bernard (Ben) E. Weber, Sr. (1880-1954) had two children, Bernard Weber II and Mary Elizabeth Weber. Mary Elizabeth had two children, Sylvia Knapp Willey and Kay Elizabeth Willey. Sylvia spent one summer at Golden Heart with my father, and recalls picking blueberries with him in the garden and listening to Thomas Furlong entertaining them in the living room at his grand piano, the two cousins seated on an antique horsehair settee, both uncomfortable and restless. When Sylvia arrived at Golden Heart to stay the week, she had been sleeping in the back seat of the car, on the drive to the farm. The young girl awoke to her great-aunt-Wilhelmina Weber, and became startled by this large heavily clothed woman, looking in at her from outside the car. To a small eight-year-old, the figure of a large unknown woman surely must have been a surprise. This was her first and only encounter with the artist, as she would never see her again.

Golden Heart Farm House, 1921

The couple held young people in high esteem. Shaping the minds of youth in the arts was a desire both shared. The Art Students League, Champlain College, and New York University were some of the groups Golden Heart retreat served. Wilhelmina Weber took the life of a student artist very seriously and she often put great effort into each of them. Close personal attention was given to them as she helped them form an individual style. Weber did everything she could to promote her students and their careers, at times often vigorously. Her studio was a place to teach still-life. Each student had a table to work from with wonderful things strewn about. She started with form and color, and progressed to simple design and layout with a rough drawing on the canvas. She was bold and confident in her studio classroom at all times. Much of the flair was in her clothing and technique as she began the lesson for the day.

In support of their teaching, Thomas Furlong and Wilhelmina Weber had a successful advertising campaign. They posted an advertisement on the schools' bulletin boards throughout their lifetime. They would place advertisements in newspapers and local publications. They held outdoor exhibitions with their students at Golden Heart and collected many works from their circle of friends. They were very much a part of the community of Bolton Landing.

Golden Heart would become a place for them to escape New York City life. Throughout the season the couple would relax and paint every summer, while teaching those who came with Wilhelmina from the League or from New York University with Thomas Furlong. We can envision the hallways of these fine institutions containing these postings for all to read for so many years. The Furlongs did make the journey to Golden Heart whenever they could, especially for exceptional friends, or special events, of which there were many.

Direct Quote From The Original Posting:

"GOLDEN HEART FARM is situated on the top of a mountain --- in the midst of a multitude of mountaintops ------ Down below Golden Heart, lies Lake George --- which is said by travelers to be the most beautiful lake in the world --- Hundreds of islands play on its sapphire surface and balloon sailing clouds mirror themselves as they pass ------ At all hours of the day and on moonlight nights, the spell of the lake contemplation leads one into new and calm lanes of peaceful enjoyment.

The pleasant old Farm House and picturesque farm buildings have been converted by the artist and his wife into simple happy interiors – which delight them --- and their old English china -- and patch quilts and little old piano in the Drawing Room. The bedrooms in the farm house are simple -- sweet smelling -- immaculately clean -- and beautiful – and colorful dormitory arrangements are in the Farm Buildings -- Everyone will be comfortable, delighted with the simplicity. The sincerity of the art expression in the house, and corral -- but the warning is ------ A primitive quality lingers -- which we love -- and will always retain -- no electricity -- no private baths! Those who are looking for "Smartness" --- for much frock changing -- for veranda gossip -- Bridge -- Bohemianism ------ WARNING!   Do not come here.

The life here is real - wholesome - complete in its naturalness -- Work and study, the response to the mountain -- to the forest -- to the magical lake ------ and relaxation that comes from complete freedom.

The delight in excellent food which is prepared under the direction of the artist's wife – (The vegetables are grown in our own garden and the milk from our cows.) ------ The informality – and, the color and general aesthetic enjoyment in the simple serving of the food ------ and the enthusiastic and pleasant dissertations and discussions during the dinner --and often out on the green sward in the early evening for further dissertations -- or playful pageantry -- or music or walks in the moonlight. Sleeping in the simple little bedrooms – or on cots under the starry sky, give such a tonic to existence at Golden Heart – that in a week the most tired and jaded city person blossoms into new life.

The great barn has been converted into a STUDIO --- there will be painting indoors and out --- on our farm of a hundred acres there are a thousand fascinating and coaxing compositions to be painted.

If you are interested in this vacation which begins on June 24th and ends on September 2nd ----- 10 weeks – you must communicate with us at once. The terms for this wonderfully constructive 10 weeks are at the rate of $25.00 a week --- $250.00 for ten weeks ------ $50.00 payable at the time of registration -- when you send in your name --- $100.00 on arrival, Balance due – July 29th --- if instruction is desired, an added fee of $50.00 for the 10 weeks is necessary --- Paid on arrival.

In addition to the numerous diversions of Golden Heart --- Riding Horses may be had --- canoes, launches at the lake --- and bathing and water sports, trout fishing, hikes, mountain climbing! --- The village is one and one-half miles from Golden Heart – For further information, write to:

GOLDENHEART FARM

BOLTON LANDING-ON-LAKE GEORGE

NEW YORK"

This detailed description of the colony is in the couple's own words. The posting, typed on a single, age-stained sheet of paper gives us insight into the life of the Furlongs while at Golden Heart for a season of fun and stress-free personal growth. This advertisement is one of the many treasures of the collection from Golden Heart Farm that offer us insight to the way of life for those who lived within its boundaries.

Golden Heart Farmhouse 1921

Pictured Magdelina Meyer Weber, Wife of August C. Weber

On display are the quilts and colorful bedspreads from Golden Heart. One in particular was amazingly colorful with bright earth tones. Inside, the floors were shiny hard wood and her art lined the walls and hallways of the farmhouse. The exterior of the house was painted, a clear luxury during that time. They took daily walks and spent entire days outside during the less harsh New England months. They painted and conversed, solving the world's problems, at one point or another, at the colony retreat. History, society, and art were the topics of many events, during the American modernist movement, roughly from 1910 to 1950. Golden Heart Farm was a gathering place for the practice of modernism in the American art world before the movement's recognition for its significant contributions.

Dorothy Dehner and David Smith

In 1926 at Golden Heart, a young twenty-six year-old student named Dorothy Dehner would spend a great deal of time with Weber before and after the death of Wilhelmina Weber's husband. Dorothy was twenty-three years younger than Weber who had been a strong mentor figure to Dorothy and David Smith. Dorothy would relax in the living room of Golden Heart often all day. The youthful couple had a very important relationship with the Furlongs. To them, the Furlongs were sophisticated people who had a well-refined way about themselves and they were very close friends. They enjoyed their time at Golden Heart. With added support and instruction of Thomas and Weber at the Art Students League, the Smith's careers blossomed together during an important time. David was a very meticulous student and friend who had done much for the Furlongs. Weber admired the young couple for their hard work and was very pleased how well their careers had done because of it. She had almost immediately recognized the couple's talent at the Art Students League. David Smith's Terminal Iron Works studio in Bolton Landing grew to a prominent place for Dorothy and David years later.

Dorothy Dehner was a student of Thomas and Weber in New York at the 3 Washington Square studio documented by Jerry Dodge in 1952. This relationship went on for many years throughout their life together. Clearly, the interaction with many in their circle was that of a community of contemporaries with much more in common than that of student and teacher. They would embrace the modernism movement because of their combined efforts. In 1965, the Smithsonian Archives of American art in Washington, DC highlighted this relationship with the Furlong's in the Dorothy Dehner oral history interviews.

Beginning in 1926 through circa 1930 while studying at the Art Students League, David Smith and the Furlongs interacted with artists John Graham, Rockwell Kent, Kimon Nicolades, Willem De Kooning and numerous others at the 3 Washington Square studio of Thomas and Weber Furlong. This time together was the formative years for many successful modernists who would emerge during the following decade of the early American modernist movement. The early period of the movement ended in the mid 1930's. Modernists of this movement would continue to test the boundaries of the socially acceptable norm well into the 1950's. This in itself is the age-old definition of avant-garde.

Dorothy and David convinced the Furlongs to purchase an automobile upon the Smith's arrival to Bolton Landing after Weber helped find them a suitable nearby location for their home. Weber was very skilled at arranging things for people throughout her life - people knew this. Professor James Kettlewell remembers the story about Dorothy and David convincing the Furlongs to purchase the automobile with the understanding the couple would teach the Furlongs how to drive. After many months of lessons, the Furlongs never mastered a driving skill. At that point, the car became a community car between the two couples. Dorothy and David eventually purchased the car and continued to drive them around whenever Thomas and Weber needed assistance.

The merry "community automobile" was purchased in July 1929 from the Hudson Motor Company of New York for $135.00, with a $25.00 deposit. It was a 1925 black Dodge Brothers Sedan, previously owned by Mr. Benjamin J. Flynn. The motorcar company was the distributor of Hudson and Essex motorcars. The new car listed for $500.00. Wilhelmina Weber inquired about a trade-in for a dark blue 1930 Ford Tudor, from the family business of D. E. Pasco and Sons, hardware, grain, and automobiles, in Warrensburg, New York on April 9, 1930. The offer she declined was for $593.00, or $202.00 down, and $36.00 per month, for 12 months. In her later years, Wilhelmina Weber did not own an automobile. Driving was a skill she was never able to master, more than likely because of her poor eyesight.

In the years before they acquired the automobile, a young girl by the name of Theta Swinton recalls the many artists that visited Golden Heart, would walk down the road past her house on their way into town down a steep incline.

During a very pleasant and emotional interview, she shared these fond memories; the Currie Family lived just down the road from the colony. Theta remembered her mother always noticed them, and noted that her mother would say, "There goes those Bohemians again," when they would walk past. The group was often-times quite large and hard to miss. At that time, there were many things to do in downtown Bolton Landing. The Curries saw the group of artists on the piers near the ferry and at the general store purchasing groceries. In her later years, Theta became a close friend to Dorothy Dehner, and the two shared many memorable times together. Theta still lives in the family home near Golden Heart Farm.

Theta's husband Tom recalls a story from the days during the Depression, when Weber and Thomas were so short on cash that on Christmas, the two could not purchase gifts. It was Christmas of 1929 and Thomas walked Weber down to the nearby creek where the couple gathered water; with their colorful house quilts spread about at the rock wall adjacent to the creek, they sat hand in hand, bundled up and warm together. Thomas had made a cozy fire to set the moment as one to remember. Apologizing for the difficulties the couple was enduring, he pointed to the beautiful noisy running water below. Romantically he gave the creek to her as a Christmas present saying "from this day forward your creek will be called Christmas Creek." After the couple returned to the house Thomas serenaded his wife with a piano concerto. For countless years after that, many of the local residents of Bolton Landing called the creek "Christmas Creek."

The late 1920s were significant years for Wilhelmina Weber at the Art Students League. Prior to her departure from the League, a decade later Weber used her skills to assist the Smiths and many other artists to promote their work. David Smith gave the Furlongs the man and woman woodcut print during a stay with them at the retreat. David Smith had made the gift of his student work as part of his initial visit from Manhattan; it is an important work.

Dorothy painted a "Portrait of Wilhelmina Weber" seated at Golden Heart in 1931 while studying at the Art Students League, which was later featured in 1987 at an exhibition called, "Art Students League Selections from the Permanent collection." The noteworthy work is now part of the permanent collection at the Heckscher Museum. The Gallery Association of New York State highlights this portrait in "The Art Students League of New York, a Permanent Collection" catalogue published in 1987. My father gave Dorothy Dehner a painting by Dorothy that was among Wilhelmina Weber's belongings upon her death.

Weber Furlong 1952

Thomas and Weber during a picnic, ca. 1921

With Wilhelmina Weber's mother Magdelina (Maggie)

Her father A.C. Weber took this photo shortly after they purchased the farm in 1921. The Furlongs had outdoor picnics quite often, during the late spring the mountaintop at Golden Heart was very pleasant. Visitors like the Smiths and relatives enjoyed the countryside. It was in this setting that their many friends would come to take pleasure in their company while staying at the art colony. Open fire cookouts and outdoor art instruction was on the agenda every spring and summer. On hillside and mountaintop, things were always happening for those who visited Thomas and Weber. Shortly after the Furlongs met the Smiths, Thomas and Weber would suffer difficult times because of the Great Depression. However, farm life made it more bearable. Weber even painted on her lovely dishtowels at that point in time, unable to purchase canvas. She would also multi task her canvasses during this time.

John Graham

Among their closest friends was the artist John Graham (1881-1961), the Ukraine-born Russian-American who at that time considered himself a modernist. Originally named Ivan Gratianovitch Dombrowsky he was from Kiev. He and Weber studied an eclectic form of minimalism together in the late 1920s. He created a rather large work purely in this minimalist style during one of his trips to Paris. Most of his work was rather small in comparison and much more eclectic. Being so closely beholden to Weber, he gave his best example of this style to her before he departed America. Here we see this wonderful gift.

John Graham, Paris, 1928

John Graham, Paris, 1927

He shared a love of Mexico City with Wilhelmina Weber, which influenced some of his art. The two shared studies at the 3 Washington Square studio in New York, where they all helped one another. Throughout her life, Weber formed groups of artists who she wished to be in a common environment. This philosophy became a method of teaching that encouraged young up-and-coming artists to thrive. The study group at 3 Washington Square was rather large and consisted of many great New York artists. Visitors to the Studio would include Willem De Kooning and Stuart Davis, both admirers of John Graham. It was in this environment she had taken her beloved Thomas under her wing as she nurtured his career throughout his life.

Graham even flirted with Native American art, a contrast seen in the gift to the Furlongs of the oil on canvas "Cultural Americas." He was somewhat endeared to Guatemala, as seen in the portrait of the "Guatemalan Woman," another gift to the Furlongs that he painted in Paris.

Graham painted one of his famous paintings of women at Golden Heart during his time with Thomas Furlong and Wilhelmina Weber. We know this because it was a gift to them during his stay at Golden Heart, sometime between 1921 and 1925. Graham gave the Furlongs four paintings at various times during his time with them. Three of the paintings were created in Paris, and the remaining one at Golden Heart. This Golden Heart portrait of Wilhelmina done by Graham was in his early years in the United States with Wilhelmina Weber as the subject.

Graham's February 25, 1937 original book number 339 published in Paris with pages uncut of Systems and Dialectics of Art are in the archives, and have been put on view with the Wilhelmina Weber Collection traveling exhibit. Evidence of their friendship has survived intact, so that all can appreciate the artistic bond that the two shared for numerous years.

John Graham bonded with Wilhelmina because she had lived in Mexico City for seven years, and he was interested in the cultures within Mexico. She influenced him deeply, and she was the subject of several paintings. It was through the Furlongs that Graham would meet Dorothy Dehner and David Smith. The Smiths and the Grahams would eventually purchase farms in Bolton Landing. They shared quite a bit of time together at Golden Heart. The Furlongs would spend time with the Smiths and the Grahams at their farms. They painted and studied with Wilhelmina Weber on several occasions during their stay, as that was the primary reason artists visited Golden Heart. The Furlongs introduced both the Grahams and the Smiths to Louis Henri Jean Charlot (1898 - 1979), while living in New York. To understand the colony and the relationships the Golden Heart artists had with each other, we look to the fact that to Wilhelmina Weber, Dorothy Dehner David Smith, and John Graham had been like family.

John Graham's portrait of Wilhelmina Weber
1921-1925

This classic John Graham portrait on display is a product of his early life in New York while working with Wilhelmina Weber, painted at a time when he was actively promoting cubism and Modern Art. The two shared thoughts on art and spirituality. One can imagine technique and form being a common interest of both artists at this time. This was a very significant friendship within the art community of the time.

Wilhelmina Weber's Modernism Emerges

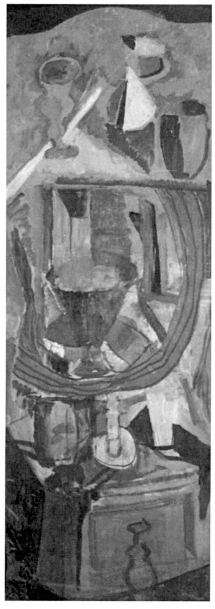

Triptych Mural, ca. 1898-1906 a great work of American art well ahead of its time.

Wilhelmina Weber was born eighteen years into the global Modernist movement, in 1878. By this time, the trends had begun that led her to become America's first avant-garde early American woman Modern Artist. American artists also pursued the movement to Europe beginning about 1860. She had become experimental with her work by 1897, at the age of nineteen, in New York. She was encouraged to develop her own style. She painted in response to a changing world, a world that was becoming modern. She thrived in the period of high modernism (1910-1930). Prior to that, she would be learning, traveling, and painting almost daily developing skills that in today's light have made her a great early American woman artist. She has earned a place in art history, and in international art communities everywhere as one of America's great Modern Artists.

In the single surviving life-size Triptych mural section, we see elements of intense confusion, meant to leave one in a state of wonder, mixed with angular still-life, and almost hinting a window or doorway to the imaginary. The other two sections have been lost to time. It is a very early work, painted between 1906 and 1918. This is a very large work well ahead of its time and full of life. Truly, this piece is a Wilhelmina Weber crown jewel. The detailed modern mix of styles seen in it are ones which cause a person to stare for quite some time at it, from near and from afar. An expert graduate student could write a thesis about Weber using this single work as a starting point.

Like many before her, Wilhelmina Weber's experience with French Impressionism allowed her to experience light itself, by actually becoming one with the pallet in the environment. The exterior world, Golden Heart Farm, became her grand studio, which allowed her to see light, without distraction, rather than an isolated object. This is evident in her landscape "Pallet at Bolton Landing" where the pallet comes directly out into the world of the artist. We see the abstract, we see impressionism, we see romanticism and we see linear cubism in several of her works. We do see a hint of post-impressionism in several of her works from Golden Heart and earlier. However, if you were to ask her about her art at that time, she would describe it as impressionistic in nature. She was developing close bonds to American avant-garde artists early in the modernist movement.

> Wilhelmina Weber experienced a deep bond with the Russian American avant-garde artist John Graham and with his culture.

Wilhelmina Weber's work displays innovative exploration with clarification of an emotional experience. Some are simple yet somewhat structured to appear sophisticated. Her works vary, many show sophistication, and many show transparency, and are easy to understand. This exploration takes place by the end of World War I and her life in Mexico City. At this point, she transitions to a life in New York's finest art community, Greenwich Village, and once again to the Art Students League. We can see the influence of her great instructors on her work, but we see her clearly defined and pleasingly unique style, described by Professor James Kettlewell in earlier papers he authored about Wilhelmina Weber and her art. The professor explains, "It was her artwork that drew me to meet her that had never happened before I was never interested in meeting an artist".

She was beginning to form a local or regional movement and to popularize it, transitioning marvelously from a third world cultural environment to an urban cultural environment. She displays the international styles of modernism, and social regionalism, which combine with an almost agrarian vision in her "Saint Swithin's Tool House" oil-on-canvas painting. However, this style seems to be somewhat short-lived, as the Jazz Age approached. It is interesting she would choose the English St. Swithin's Day for the title of this painting. Upon closer examination, this is the day of weather for the Saxon Bishop of Winchester (852-862), when people watch the weather for forty days during mid-summer. This painting represents a clear and profound message of high modernism, with angular representations and rural overtones from the life of the artist, much like the life she enjoyed. Furthermore, additional study reveals there is an English rhyme for Saint Swithin's feast holiday:

St. Swithin's day if thou dost rain
For forty days it will remain
St. Swithin's day if thou be fair
For forty days 'twill rain nae mair

Saint Swithin's Tool House 1923 it represents the artists' interpretation of life at Golden Heart Farm for it bears the name of Wilhelmina Weber's most beloved Little House.

Fortunately, at Golden Heart she resisted the consumer culture, which transformed modernism as a movement to what we now know is the postmodern movement. Rather interesting is the period of the élite modernist she was clearly a participant. With that said, this made her the first early American woman modernist with abundant work so clearly defined and understood by the historian's and collectors of her region. The early American modernists painted from (1910-1950). This membership was a small handful of artists, who brought the movement to the forefront, many of whom she had known quite well. Men dominated the movement in near totality; a woman artist at her level was an unusual occurrence, especially one so well- traveled, and so well-educated in the artistic schools of thought. Rare though it was, we are fortunate her father allowed her to develop her pursuits from so young an age, with the support of her family and teachers, beginning in 1890, twenty years prior to the period of the élite early American modernist. Her work is clearly ahead of its time and the expressionistic character of her work is unmistakable.

She also flourished forty years later, from 1930 through 1940. Wilhelmina Weber was a part of the progressive changes that had begun to dominate modernism. This was a progressive period for American thought and for the American Modernists. It was in this period that the problem-solving viewpoints artists held took front and center at the art colony of Golden Heart Farm. Her art during this period took on the defined socialist overtone, with the raised fist rising over the table of a once civil still life. In this oil-on-canvas painting, titled "The Ostrich Egg," her still-life becomes part of a bigger picture, of varying American cultures, dominated by multi-cultural images, clearly on the fringe of acceptability.

For Weber, this bold image was a very clear message of social or political revolution. It represents equality brought to the still-life tabletop, which fed Russian and Mexican society at that time. Modernists began to emerge in support of economic democracy. In relation, bear in mind that Wilhelmina Weber was a close friend of John Graham, the Russian born painter, and she had lived through the Mexican Revolution in southern Mexico. Many artists at that time believed the Russian Revolution was an answer to the progressive dream Modernists desired. Unfortunately, the dream was lost in Russia, when Stalin put an end to the freedom of ideas artists so universally desired. Graham had suffered immense hardships in Russia during the Revolution, when the Bolsheviks had him imprisoned in 1918 for his participation as a counter-revolutionary, after the assassination of Czar Nicholas II and his family. It was this reality our early American modernist Wilhelmina Weber knew all too well by her first-hand, real life experience in Cuernavaca, Mexico during the height of the Mexican Revolution.

Bold Imagery of the Ostrich Egg, ca. 1923's

Modern still-life, ca. 1913-1920

At this point, it is important to note that Wilhelmina Weber did not participate in the socialist version of realism that began to emerge after World War II. This is often confused with social realism in art during the Great Depression, which we do see a hint of in her work, however short-lived it might have been.

Thomas Furlong, on the other hand, painted such works, as a muralist during his long tenure in Chicago, with Mr. Oliver Gould Jennings, at Bethlehem Steel. His images of the working class in the steel factory express a common social realism of the time, the portrayal of the daily way of life for the working person. These works of art were set in an industrial steel and ironworker's environment, and were a special commissioning by Jennings for his industrial unit. Thomas designed brilliant advertising copy and modern graphic art material for packaging supplies used by the industrialist. His talent as a graphic artist was paramount for the time. He painted a realist portrait of the industrialist, which hung at the headquarters of Bethlehem Steel for many years.

Portrait of Wilhelmina by Thomas Furlong, ca. 1911-1912

The prestigious Hyde Collection in Glens Falls, New York, has a distinguished portrait of Wilhelmina Weber in its collection painted by Thomas Furlong. Wilhelmina cherished another portrait of herself, painted by her loving husband Thomas Furlong, which was shown at the Marfa Building 98 exhibition of 2012. This particular portrait was a favorite of my father's. We featured it on the advertisement for the exhibition of her paintings at Building 98 in Marfa. Amazingly, there is a very early modern painting on the back of this portrait, because at this period in their life, times were tough, and they could not spend money on canvases. After the crash of the stock market and the losses of two world wars, artists learned to conserve, and this was one way to accomplish more with less. It adds mystery to the artist's work. The Wilhelmina Weber Collection has several overpaints and reverse side paintings as evidence of this.

Reverse side of portrait, painted ca. 1898-1904 by Weber

For many years, I never looked behind the portrait of Wilhelmina that had hung on our walls throughout my lifetime. This was the most emotional painting the family had of our grand aunt. Whenever my father would tell us stories, it was always in front of the painting the dialogue would begin. I looked forward to the stories my father would tell on these special occasions. On the reverse side was this very early modern work hidden from view my entire life.

Glens Falls and Bolton Landing

Wilhelmina Weber was a part of the Glens Falls and Bolton Landing communities throughout most of her life. She survived through her artistic talents by teaching the art of painting to many adults and children in the region. Her work in Bolton Landing led the school board to engage an art teacher in 1954. This was a result of her students holding an exhibit at the Bolton Bank on June 8, 1953, which was one of a series of exhibits throughout the region that year. An estimated 500 people viewed 150 paintings at the first annual Bolton Landing art exhibition. Her students were from Bolton Landing, Lake George, Glens Falls, Fort Edward, and Warrensburg.

Art instruction led her to an association with Charlotte Hyde and Jerry Dodge from 1941 to 1962. Jerry took an interest in Wilhelmina Weber's art and became a devoted friend. Thanks to generous benefactors like Charlotte Hyde, she was able to teach and sell much of her artwork in Glens Falls, New York. Another of her Glens Falls benefactors was Mrs. Ruth Fratus, the wife of Earl T. Fratus. Ruth was one of Wilhelmina Weber's closest friends, and became a friend of my mother Mitzi Weber Royer. The couple would take the Furlongs on boat rides on their yacht on Lake George, and on occasion Ruth took my mother and father with them. It was in letters from Ruth we found local news articles about Wilhelmina Weber's art. Also of mention are Jane and Dick Hopkins of Glens Falls, and the artist Jerry Dodge, who assisted with her needs by supporting her work as an artist.

In Glens Falls, Wilhelmina Weber had a group that met in her studio, from what I can tell, each day. There were fourteen members of the group. Known as The Circle Studio, they arrived at 10:00 AM and departed by 12:00 Noon. This kept her very busy. Her friend, Professor James Kettlewell, reveals that she lived in a small 1840s house in downtown Glens Falls where he met her many times. The owner, a local lawyer by the name of Robert Le Pann permitted her to live on his property by accepting paintings as a form of rent. Just next-door was the law office of Le Pann and Reardon. While living at this small Victorian home, Weber revealed some insight into her life. She wrote:

"I never lost a day in the Circle Studio -

Do then the preparations for the day –

It takes a lot out of you, to put up the gay window dressings -

We're ready - It was always way after midnight."

In a letter dated July 3, 1957, Wilhelmina writes:

"I have moved to Golden Heart, and in the late autumn, will have a working studio in Glens Falls, on the ground floor, the two long flights of stairs were too much for a member of the Circle Studio."

She writes; concerning Mom bringing a small newborn baby my sister, Anjea Weber now deceased, with her to Golden Heart Farm:

"I don't recommend the hardships of our mere mountaintop in its present neglect, as a suitable place for a little baby, the principal bottle neck being water, which we have to carry 720 feet. It is warm in the spring."

Among her students in the early 1950s in Glens Falls, New York, we located Eleanor Elliott and Bell Drew. The two took classes together after reading about her studio in the *Glens Falls Times*. Wilhelmina Weber had run an advertisement and the two thought it would be fun to take classes together. We met Eleanor Elliott at the Crandall public library after she read about our first public presentation in Glens Falls. Before the event started she announced, "I was a student of Wilhelmina Weber Furlong. I studied under a famous artist." After our initial meeting, she telephoned to say that she brought three paintings down from her attic that she had painted. They had resided there for sixty-three years. Eleanor's paintings showed the influence of her great teacher. We noticed Eleanor had begun to add extra paint for more texture to the still-life she had created. We gained insight into Wilhelmina Weber's teaching style from Eleanor as she described Weber's studio and the objects she had painted. "As students, we often worked alone to progress developing a unique form and style of our own".

During Weber's final years in Glens Falls from 1952 to 1962, Dorothy Dehner tended to her on a somewhat regular basis. Dorothy would be with her in the house on Elm Street and the upstairs studio on 25 Ridge Street. She would come from New York and stay, often overnight. Dorothy greeted Weber's students from the Circle Studio group on numerous occasions at the studio, while visiting Weber. However, these visits became less frequent after Dorothy moved to New York and became very busy with exhibitions of her own art. This was after her time as a student at Skidmore College.

At this time, Weber, communicated with Alfred H. Barr Jr., the founder of MOMA in Manhattan, for assistance on a book, he had published called, "*What is Modern Painting*". The letter is on microfiche at the museum archives.

Kingston Daily Freeman, the newspaper in Kingston, NY, published an article on January 4, 1962, after legislators turned the main corridors of the New York State Assembly hall into an art gallery to highlight regional artists. "Assemblyman Richard J. Bartlett, R-Glens Falls, sponsored paintings by sculptor David Smith and Elsa Steinback of Bolton Landing, and Weber Furlong, Shirley Patton, Irving Juster, Joseph J. Dodge, Tom Mcintosh and Douglass Crockwell all of Glens Falls."

As Weber's eyesight failed to near blindness, only seeing in bright light, she could still see the stunning sunset, according to my mother Mitzi. In her transition to blindness, one can see the variance in her works from beginning to end. Her students said, "Some of her most inspiring work was during the time of her failing eyesight" and "she always enjoyed and appreciated the work of those around her." Eventually, she became legally blind, but she continued to paint and paint quite well, though often unable to pay for canvas. Wealthy friends who loved both her and her art tended to help her. I learned she would throw pennies away because she could not identify them. My mother tried to give her a handful of them, which she had left behind on a dresser, and she quickly refused them. Before her death, parts of her holdings were still intact, and she possessed priceless works of art and antiques. My father sold the small portion of land remaining, to George Barber and some of her larger belongings he gave to her friends. She had been indebted to a few who cared for her during her last days.

Today, the New York community of Bolton Landing still holds her in very high esteem. A short biography of Thomas Furlong and Wilhelmina Weber at the Bolton Landing Chamber Of Commerce website elaborates on an initial 1919 visit to the Bremestead Private School for girls, where the two painted the tearoom together. They were both socially active and charitable. The Bremestead School at that time maintained a scholarship fund for children, and was a favorite project for Madame Louise Homer (1871-1947), the great singer from the Metropolitan Opera in New York. That season, in the early fall of 1919, Homer would be performing at the school for a dinner, bazaar, and fundraiser for the children. She performed the Mother Goose Songs, illustrated by live performance of tableaux and pantomime. The tearoom was the venue for the magnificent event. The previous year, Madame Homer had sung the "Star-Spangled Banner" for a Fourth of July celebration on Lake George. Like the Furlongs, Madame Homer enjoyed the region as a summer retreat. The Furlongs participated in numerous events like this in New York and at their home in Bolton Landing, which they purchased two years later. It was Madame Louise Homer, who had first introduced Weber Furlong to the community of Bolton Landing. This close association afforded Weber access to Manhattan society. Beginning in 1913 Weber Furlong provided brightly decorated opera set furniture, to salon performances. One in particular was the revival performance of "Mlle.Modiste" at the Globe Theater. Weber's Three Washington Square North Studio called the "*Yellow Shop*" had originally been located at 122 E. 59th Street in Manhattan.

Upon her death in 1962, my father gave much of her artwork to those who assisted her financially, as patrons of her art. Without them, she would have never survived on her own. Some of that work is at the prestigious Hyde Collection museum in Glens Falls. It was noted at an exhibition there from April 16 to May 31, 1966, that many of her private collectors also studied and worked with her. This was important to her. Weber had become a remarkable artist in the city. This was her post-New York City community. They fulfilled her life, and interacted daily with her. The city had created a remarkable artist. The Hyde Collection exhibition revealed the great extent that locals in the region of Glens Falls and Bolton Landing admired her. The 1966 published list of collectors and paintings totals thirty-nine, and contains works by Thomas Furlong.

Throughout her life, Wilhelmina Weber was deeply enriched by her love of modernism through the expression of her art, a fact known well to her family and the communities, which she served.

Wilhelmina Weber's 25 Ridge Street 2nd floor Glens Falls, studio and apartment, as seen in 1957

She passed away in a small private studio apartment in Glens Falls, surrounded by her artist friends and caregivers. She only retained a small portion of Golden Heart land, where her ashes were scattered. I know my father was deeply saddened by her death. He respected her last wishes and he unknowingly paved the way for this exhibition by allowing me to admire the art from such a young age. The effect she had on his life was unmistakable.

During her final days, those who cared for her took handwritten notes on her thoughts or mood at the time. They helped her to make handwritten memos, words like "the snow falls, the green grass grows" were legible. The most moving are some of Wilhelmina's less coherent hand written notes, one containing only the date 1913. What was the significance to her of the date 1913? Another memo is what I believe to be a final wish, one I would eventually fulfill by writing this biography. It reads "The Book of Thomas (Tomas) Furlong St. Louis 1886 -1952 and Weber. Mary Wilhelmina Weber Furlong, St Louis 1878 – "

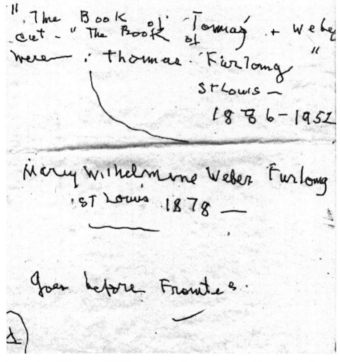

This handwritten 1962 memo is among the most moving

The next morning after finding the memos, I awoke very early, realizing that in 1913 Wilhelmina Weber left Mexico.

I realized she had met Thomas (Tomas) in Mexico between 1911 and 1912, so it was clear. This was the year the story of Thomas and Weber had begun. That year, she was to return to the city she loved, New York, with the man that she loved, Thomas Furlong. The couple had left Mexico City together, opened a studio and Gallery at 122 E. 59th Street, and had begun their shared life with each other. Within one year, the couple had a successful gallery and an active social life that led them to the most prestigious circles of American Modernism. The two were professional partners in life and they remained together un-married for several years. The life of an artist was indeed a difficult one, and on occasion Wilhelmina Weber would be on the receiving end of a scolding from Thomas Furlong's sister before they were married.

In her letters to her brother, Ella D. Dawson would write that she would regret scolding her, but felt Weber understood why she had chastised her. The bold letters did not elaborate on the specific issue but one need only look to the fact the couple had been living together before they married. This in itself was very progressive for the time. The progressive movement was flourishing from 1890 to 1930 in the United States and the Furlong's were very much a part of the movement.

Most of the works of Thomas Furlong that were given to the Dreyfuss family with the understanding they were to do what they could to make Thomas Furlong famous since they were among her dearest friends. As an example of this close bond with the family, Dr. William Dreyfuss was given custody of Weber's ashes for them to be scattered at Golden Heart when the family arrived from Texas. The Dreyfuss family had spent time at Golden Heart with the Furlongs during the beautiful Bolton landing summer months and there was a great deal of respect for Dr. Dreyfuss for all he had done for Weber.

To her in-laws, she pushed things to the limit with extended family members. They could not understand her innovative ideas. Wilhelmina Weber alternatively may have seemed somewhat surreal to them. She was older than her husband was, and she had spent a great deal of time with Thomas before they were married. The family, except my father, who loved her dearly, did not fully understand Wilhelmina Weber. The immediate family seemed to focus on the greatness of Thomas Furlong rather than that of Wilhelmina Weber. This perception was one she herself had fostered.

My father was very close to Aunt Wilhelmina (Minnie), and stayed with them yearly from an early age, after the premature death of his father, Bernard E. Weber II. In the mid-1930s as a young boy, he loved his time at Golden Heart Farm, and he met many of the people who passed through the art colony between 1936 and 1952. In adulthood, his aunt Minnie would often write to him saying, "Golden Heart was always seen and understood from his young teenage eyes better than anyone else." He always comprehended its intrinsic value, which he instilled in me through our many lengthy conversations about life at Golden Heart. When dad would talk about Golden Heart, he would often become visibly emotional. His love for Minnie was profound, rooted in her lifelong love of art and the love she held for Thomas, and the way the couple lived their life together. Dad would tell me, that hers was a life without worry, a life without anger, and a life without personal wealth. These thoughts made my father very happy, and indeed, they represented some of the happiest days of his teenage life.

To her second-generation family she was nicknamed "Aunt Minnie." After her death, the art collection of Wilhelmina Weber came into the possession of my father Bernard E. Weber III, the only Weber namesake relative of Wilhelmina Weber, since they bore no children. The collection became mine while my father was still alive. I have kept the paintings in my home, with the bulk of them under my bed, for over forty-one years. Amazingly, the entire Wilhelmina Weber Collection survived the destruction of Hurricane Katrina in New Orléans after a midnight evacuation of the entire inventory.

I was in my early teens when my father (Ben) would tell me about his time at Bolton Landing with Thomas Furlong and Wilhelmina Weber. He told me that the artists could be seen painting inside and outside on a regular basis, as the colony compound was quite large. The Lake George countryside speaks for itself. Dad would roam the countryside, and wade in the creeks throughout the farm. Fishing with his Aunt Minnie was one of his favorite pastimes as a young boy, and she taught him how to clean the fish. In turn, he taught me. It was during times such as this he would share her life with me. For me this was very significant and it gave me a better understanding of life for the many artists of Golden Heart and of our grand aunt.

Wilhelmina's brother, Bernard with whom she was very close, handed down a memorable poem (author unknown), and it went like this:

> "Carve not thy name in stone or wood, that I was neither bad nor good, but remember seven words and the words are these, He lived he loved and he understood."

My mother tells me that Wilhelmina Weber's brother Bernard Weber would tease Wilhelmina about her long hair, pulled back in a bun with strands whisking over the side of her face. "Minnie" he would proclaim, "Why don't you pull that hair from your face?" Throwing her head sideways and grabbing it with her hand, she would reply, "but it is my artist identity." One might conclude from this dazzling description of her that Wilhelmina had a manner about herself that for those days was somewhat stylish. She expressed her love of the arts in her painting as well as with her mannerisms. She had mastered her bold entry into the room at an event or party often with large flowing and colorful garments draped around her and usually wearing something over her head; be it a large hat or her signature beret.

Glens Falls, New York 1956

Mother remembers this most and recalls Wilhelmina Weber always wore a beret on her head, slanted sideways. This well-known beret is in the portrait on display in the Weber Furlong Collection and in numerous photographs.

The Modern Day Adventure

I was two years old on May 26, 1962, when Wilhelmina Weber passed away at the age of eighty-three. The year before, she held me in her arms joyfully, since she never was able to bear children. As the only grandson, and the only boy in a family of all girls, I survived all the ear tugging the women in the family would give me, not to mention all the extra attention. From Glens Falls, New York, the Weber Furlong Collection traveled to San Antonio, Texas, where my parents vigilantly cared for them for many years, packed up and sealed airtight. They moved with our family to Minnesota, Houston, Dallas, and several interim homes. In our travels, every step of the way, the paintings remained carefully tended to, stored under our beds, and packed unframed in artist folios.

When I was nine years old in 1969, I was rummaging around in the basement of our current family home. I discovered several flat cardboard boxes. They had been untouched for one year, placed there during the final family move. I carted them up into my bedroom and began the task of unpacking and looking at the contents. To my amazement, stunning, pristine oil paintings and watercolors by the dozens were before my young eyes. Colorful, majestic, and bewildering might come close to explaining my situation. The next day, I went down and found an old briefcase, with all their personal letters, writings, and photographs. To a small child, it was a treasure because of the old stamps, which I quickly collected. In reality, the piece of luggage in itself was the real treasure, full of personal effects, résumés, titles, and deeds. I had found Wilhelmina Weber's life and an extensive photographic record of the artist's life the attaché case contained!

This ritual would continue throughout my childhood. I would slide them out from under the bed, and one by one, carefully slide them from right to left, and look at each one for hours on end. At times, I would thumbtack them on the walls, and alternate them for my enjoyment. I knew then that they were important works and I enjoyed studying them. I felt at times as if someone was looking over my shoulder with me, as I viewed each one of the paintings ever so carefully. Throughout my childhood beginning at age nine, I cared for the paintings as the custodian of the life's work of one of America's great modernist painters. In my adult life, the collection of paintings also traveled with me to many places.

In the present day, I have realized the inspiration gained from this has been a very important part of my life. Oddly, as a child, I never shared them with anyone until 1999 when I began to place some of them on my walls after returning home to Texas after a long military career. The appreciation of the arts I now hold is so much a part of me that my life had been changed forever by the experience. I felt I always had her art in my life; the art of a great American woman artist linked me to the past. Today, her legacy continues as I compile the pages of this story, rediscovering my great-grand-aunt all over again as an adult.

Meeting her beloved art students and talking to those who knew her throughout New York has been a community event. Once we published news about her story, people came forward who knew her. Word spread throughout the region and the children of many of her former students still had some of Weber's belongings and her artwork. Speaking with them was an emotional experience for everyone. With their own stories to tell about Wilhelmina Weber, they had joined the project. So as a result, in 2012 or one full year into the project, we had managed to locate sixteen people outside the immediate family who had met or studied under Wilhelmina Weber Furlong. One of them, George Barber studied under Thomas Furlong. Understanding the artist and teacher Thomas Furlong is also an important part of the Wilhelmina Weber Furlong art history project.

The documentary film and its oral histories track across Lake George, Saratoga Springs, Glens Falls, Plattsburg, New York City, and Bolton Landing, New York. It was an adventure of discovery that we felt was a search for Weber so we named the project "In Search of Weber." We currently travel to Glens Falls and Bolton Landing as we prepare to exhibit Weber's work and continue the documentary project for a more complete picture of the life of Wilhelmina Weber Furlong and that of her remaining students. Seeing the work of her students also gave us insight into their renowned teacher and confidant.

We made significant contacts in Marfa, Texas at the height of our 2012 Weber Furlong project; among them, Joseph Dodge the son of the Hyde Museum curator Jerry Dodge from 1941 to 1962. Bolton town historian Ted Caldwell and his wife Jane traveled form Bolton Landing to see Weber's art in Marfa, Texas. Between September 27 and February 10 2012, the exhibit remained up for public viewing, extended by popular demand.

Discovering people with something to say about their encounters between fifty-five and sixty-five years ago only shows how important it is to grasp the project as one of extreme importance before it is too late. Equally important is the sense of joy in the life of those who knew Weber this project has brought to them. The community of people closest to Wilhelmina Weber Furlong remains impacted by her work as an elderly woman as they approach the age she was when they met her as students and close friends in the early 1950's. The woman they knew was at the completion of her life continuing to peruse her life's desire still influencing people right up to her final days in 1962. During the first year of the project, Ed Nedau one of the men we interviewed on film, passed away in Glens Falls five months later.

Wilhelmina Weber's Significant Modernist Status Earned

Who was Wilhelmina Weber Furlong? The answer is obvious. She was the first early American woman avant-garde Modern Artist. She predated the period of early American High Modernism (1910-1930) by twenty years. We are emphasizing the American period of High Modernism. European modernism had begun by 1860, and the Americans followed suit with the rest of the world to join the movement, which men dominated in near totality. We are focusing on the early modernist movement within American art. This movement was prevalent in the American Northeast. Many rejected modernism and the modernists during its infancy. Because of this, many artists struggled to stay productive during the movement. Some of America's greatest early Modern Artists revered Wilhelmina Weber, and she has earned her place as the first woman modernist in her circle of American modernists painters. During her time, people throughout the art communities she touched admired her and collected her work. She studied under some of the great painters of her time. She was an art teacher, deeply entrenched in early American academia, who instructed some of the most accomplished artists in the movement. She was an event aficionado and the life of any social gathering. It is true, that the amazing woman called Weber, always held people around her in high esteem and she did everything she could to assist her students. Wilhelmina Weber was ardently devoted to the arts in New York City for over 70 years. This history revealed in today's light is spectacular. She never looked back, and she never looked too far forward. She only lived for the moment, and in the moment. This characteristic is one that bears repeating because that was indeed her. Well-received and her history accepted within the important art community she touched Wilhelmina Weber's story has been told.

Weber Furlong Paintings Exhibited in Glens Falls

Aerie to Hold

An exhibit of paintings by Weber Furolng, a pioneer in the modern art movement in America who died in Glens Falls in 1962, continues through this month at the Hyde Art Collection, 161 Warren street, Glens Falls.

* * *

Weber Furlong made her influence for modernism felt in American painting in the late 1920s when she was executive secretary of the Art Students League in New York city, then the most advanced art school in the country.

Her art was entirely devoted to still life painting and she described her style as "expressionistic." She had strong feelings about the objects she painted, carefully collecting and saving pieces of china and glass, broken musical instruments and pots, and brightly colored pieces of cloth.

Many of these things were preserved by her students and are on exhibit at the Hyde Collection along with her paintings.

The former Wilhelmina Weber from St. Louis, she was married to Thomas Furlong, a painter who taught at New York University, Hunter College and Champlain College.

* * *

In 1921, the Furlongs purchased their farm, "Golden Heart" at Bolton Landing on Lake George.

The Furlongs introduced the late sculptor David Smith to Bolton Landing. He settled there and developed the famous metal sculpture that has ranked him among the most important sculptors of the 20th century.

In 1952, Thomas Furlong died and Weber moved to Glens Falls where she gave private lessons in art until shortly before her death in 1962.

The Hyde Collection is open Sunday, Tuesday, Wednesday and Friday from 2 to 5 p.m.

Article in the "Schenectady Gazette," May 16, 1966

The Hyde Collection in Glens Falls New York had close ties throughout the art communities of New England and New York, through the work of Jerry Dodge. In the early 1940s, Jerry and Wilhelmina shared mutual friends, and the appreciation of her still-life expressionistic yet modern style is revealed in two paintings by Wilhelmina Weber that were in the private collection of Jerry Dodge, acquired before he left Glens Falls. In the years after Jerry departed, Weber came to be well-regarded within the communities the Hyde museum served. In small steps, her circle of students and friends grew because of that, her influence remains throughout the region. Many of them picked up her unique modern style, a style she had gained only after leaving her earlier style of 1890's impressionism behind. This transition became more evident shortly after returning from France between 1898 and 1906, and was complete in New York after assuming her position at the Art Students League during the highpoint of early American Modernism between 1910 and 1930. She more than likely felt pressure much later to drop many of the early techniques she had come to embrace from her circle of friends at the League, specifically Max Weber, and to a much lesser extent, John Graham on his early arrival to the United States in 1920. Additionally, the Whitney Studio Galleries, being so prominent in her life between 1918 and 1928 before moving to Golden Heart, meant that there was a strong influence present to join the modernist movement during the movements' early days in New York. The mission of the Whitney Studio Galleries was to promote the modernist and Modern Art during the infancy of American Modernism. Thanks to these efforts, artists could express themselves in this new and rather bold art form.

Wilhelmina Weber had become devoted to the modernist philosophy and she was a very great artist in the movement for her ability to paint real objects with brilliant color and a new, more modern form that highlighted not only the object but also brought form and realism to the paint on the artist's canvas. This philosophy consumed much of the New York art landscape after the stage had been set for its conclusion years later. As a woman in New York Weber's role in this was very important, specifically at the Art Students League, 3 Washington Square, and Golden Heart Farm, as she began to lay the groundwork among American abstract artists well before the movements climax.

This makes Wilhelmina Weber a foremother to the American Modern Art movement, a role revealed by the passage of time, her significant position in New York, and the continued devotion of art historian and curator Professor Emeritus James Kettlewell of Skidmore College.

Towards the end of her life, the students of Wilhelmina Weber in Glens Falls and Bolton Landing, who dearly loved her, would become Hyde museum docents for James Kettlewell, because of these friendships. This becomes quite evident with the discovery of the 1966 article in the "Schenectady Gazette" four years after her death on the previous page. This art retrospective was the labor of Douglass Crockwell and James Kettlewell, who honored their friend with a memorial showing of her artwork and personal effects.

The artist Douglass Crockwell (1904-1968) was a very close friend of Wilhelmina Weber's, and was the Chair of the Hyde Collection Board of Trustees along with James K Kettlewell, as the new curator he was instrumental in securing a large assembly of Weber's paintings from throughout the region. Furthermore, Professor Kettlewell is responsible for most of the continued attention to Wilhelmina Weber. As a curator and art history professor, he is indisputably one of the most qualified art historians to analyze her work. The two were well-acquainted, and he was able to share many thoughts with her on art. He and his wife Lucy knew and visited Wilhelmina Weber in Glens Falls on a weekly basis. As a member of the Circle Studio group, Mrs. Lucy Kettlewell was also an artist influenced by Weber's modern style. The two-shared stories about Wilhelmina's early life for several years before Wilhelmina passed away.

There were several articles published at that time about the Hyde museum exhibit. In December after the exhibit, Jane Hopkins wrote in a letter to my mother, "for all her oddities she was a great old gal I feel my life was so greatly enriched fresh from knowing her." Jane was emotional at seeing what a great show her paintings made with that emotion she was deeply touched. Jane had assisted the exhibition with its setup and dismantling with James K. Kettlewell.

Professor Kettlewell wrote the Weber Furlong retrospective for the Hyde Collection event in 1966, and a later exhibit at Skidmore College, where he is Lecturer and Professor Emeritus of Art History. Professor James K. Kettlewell replaced John K. Howat at the Hyde Collection. John Howat only served for two years between 1962 and 1964 and James K. Kettlewell served from 1966 to 1984.

In 1994, when he was involved in a regional exhibition of local art at the Ft. Edward Art Center southeast of Glens Falls, James Kettlewell highlighted the importance of Wilhelmina Weber to the community, which still admires her to this very day. The exhibit ran from June 18, to August 19, 1994. The curator of the one-woman show "titled Weber Furlong" was Katie DeGroot, who at that time was the president of the Ft. Edward Art Center.

The Weber Furlong Foundation owes Professor James Kettlewell a huge debt of gratitude for his lifelong dedication to the art community and to Wilhelmina Weber Furlong. Without his insight into Wilhelmina, we would have been missing a vital piece of the historical puzzle to bring Wilhelmina Weber into today's perspective. After her death, the professor was unable to contact the family because of the death of Thur Krarup, the man who had shipped her life's work to Texas. Subsequently, he began a search for the family that lasted 50 years, including tasking students with the mystery of locating her paintings. However, a family on the move is rather difficult to find. One by one, they hit dead ends in the search for her paintings. Our initial introduction was one of life's meaningful experiences for all involved. It came about after I discovered Professor Kettlewell's publication from the 1966 Hyde Museum exhibit in one of Jane Hopkins' letters to my mother that same year. The correspondence contained the exhibit catalogue. From that, I set out to locate the author of that essay on Weber Furlong.

Professor Kettlewell remains a very active art historian. Because of this, he was rather easy to find. Given the fact that he published his works and that he travels the United States and Europe conducting research, all I had to do was send him an e-mail to his published website address and the rest is history.

We are fortunate to have Professor James Kettlewell's academic support of this Biography. He is very committed to the Wilhelmina Weber project and has organized academic support by preparing lectures and written material about Weber's modern style and of her importance to American Art. Between 1952 and 1962, Professor Peter Brauzzi exhibited Wilhelmina Weber's work twice at Skidmore College while the artist was still alive. The Tang Museum at Skidmore College holds a work by Weber Furlong that has been exhibited regionally since 1952. Donated to the Tang by Katie DeGroot this painting was featured at the Ft. Edward Art Center exhibit.

Professor James K. Kettlewell, on set, "In Search of Weber"
Lake George Spring of 2012

Some Important Quotes

On her talent the 1966 Hyde exhibition article in the "Glens Fall's Times" discusses her use of color:

"Color is most important and although vibrant tones have been used, they have been so skillfully balanced and integrated that one is aware only of the completed whole."

"There is little of the startling and bizarre"

On herself, Wilhelmina Weber would speak often as "not belonging to any one school," and she saw herself as an expressionist.

Wilhelmina Weber: "I start with an arrangement and then follow the mood or feeling I have at the time."

"Becoming aware of aesthetic experiences; do not see what you expect to see."

In a 1957 exhibition at Skidmore College, in Saratoga Springs New York, Adel Woodworth describes, "She is touched by form and objects and in her painting personalizes them to reveal emotion or feeling."

James K. Kettlewell writes, in 1966:

"No Modern Artist has concentrated so exclusively in still-life subjects. All of the objects Weber portrayed had for her special meanings and definite personalities."

"Weber Furlong's work belongs solidly in the Modern Art tradition.

"Weber Furlong's colors are always very strong in the manner of European Fauves and German Expressionists."

Katie DeGroot President of the Fort Edward Art Center writes, in May, 1994:

"An artist can only work hard and hope to make as permanent an impression on others as Weber did during her lifetime."

Matthew Aulicino writes in May, 1994:

"Furlong's art is part of the modern tradition in American art; her work is deeply rooted in the foundations of Modern Art displaying the ideas that directed modern American painters."

Wilhelmine Weber, a Craftswoman of The New Modernist School, Reproduces Painted Furniture Of the Russian Peasants

By YETTA DOROTHEA GEFFEN
New York Press Sunday, February 1,1914

ON **the north Side of Washington**

square, the only side where old time aristocracy still holds its own among the faithful followers of art and refuses to migrate further up town to more imposing and fashionable avenues. A single studio building raises its head a trifle above those of its neighbors. It looks out proudly over the square and boasts of its indisputable position in Washington square society. Number three is a double building, a fact that is usually discovered only when one has occasion to go to the rear half of it without being warned of its duplicity. After innocently and confidently climbing three or four flights of stairs to the very top, is one informed of his blunder and of the curious and unnatural character of the house. Whereupon, still puffing like a steam engine, you retrace your steps to the bottom, fumble halteringly through a mysterious, long hallway and, still suspicious, mount another stairway that looms up at you out of the darkness.

At the Top

When you have finally reached the breathless end of your adventurous journey, a most pleasing and musical voice confronts you. And Weber—Wilhelmine Weber—hanging over the banister, entreats you to come right up in. "In" proves to be a place so bright and sunshiny-looking, that you immediately forget the stereotyped little speeches about the gloomy weather that you had mentally conjured up as a conversation opener. So you gasp out your delight between laborious puffs and proceed to sink Into the big, low "comfy" chair that is gently pushed out toward you. You are in a place of gorgeous colors. Glowing crimson mingles with a splendid dark blue and warm yellow on lacquered surfaces which you see at once are great chests, settees, chairs and cupboards. You know that the gayest chest is probably one of the peasant "marriage chests" of which you have heard—which the modernist bride is adopting from the far-away Russian maidens, for the arduous keeping of her wedding household linen.

The Yellow Shop

It is here that Weber—unprefixed by the "Miss," as she prefers to be called—painter, artist, decorator and a recent exhibitor at the Artists Guild and Museum in St Louis, hides herself to her work. "This is my yellow workshop," she introduced. You like the name. It makes you smile, and smiles are very natural in this sunny "workshop."

It is a place of yellow walls, bright light, smiles and hard work. Weber tried further to apologize for the disordered appearance of the shop but haven't all studios an appearance of artistic disorder, she was asked?

"No indeed" she laughed. "Some are very orderly but they must be very horrid places to work in. I don't believe I could work in a place that had to be kept trim and just so. It's such a comfort to be able to kick over a can of turpentine without kicking up a fuss about it afterward."

Of all the bright scene, Weber herself was the brightest, and gayest and most picturesque part. Clad in a simple gown of antique Mexican gypsy cloth—in a design of bright red, green and yellow rows of flowers upon a background of intense purple falling in simple, severe lines from neck to heel and partially concealed by a linen smock. She seemed to gather and hold all the color in the room as she draped her tall form gracefully in a low wicker armchair. And this, in spite of the fact that the room contained several ornamental bits of Modernist hangings, a few scarf's of deep, solid colors thrown artistically over a chair and a number of gay canvases. One, a particularly happy subject of warm colors, was a decorative screen that was being done by Thomas Furlong, a friend and co-worker of Weber. Scattered about the room, oddly contrasted with the few wicker chairs, were several pieces of furniture, almost crude in their straightness and severity of line. There were a chair, a table, a big chest and a cupboard, painted a very light gray for a background, and then in the process of being decorated. This is my Russian work," she explained, "about which I am so enthusiastic about just now, but it won't look anything like this when the work will be completed." she hastened to add. "It's an adaptation of the work of Russian peasants or Monjiks, as they are called. A peasant you know, scarcely sees a piece of wood, when he feels, like splashing on it, in gay color, and swishing in lines of fascinating design. It is extraordinary how it sets your heart fluttering on seeing for the first time the jolly painted furniture of a peasant cottage. It's so filled with color, so happy and satisfying. The doors, the beams, the ceiling, the icon shrine, open cupboards, corner shelves, racks for the pottery, tables, chairs, the great wooden majestic bed, the quaint cradles, the bridal chests, and even the outline of an enormous settee of straight, box-like lines and another of a massive chair to match. I am doing this for an ultra salon de Modiste."

"The background of these chairs is a strong; Slavic blue and the upholstering, vivid cadmium yellow. The decoration is in the form of Inset panels, a painted mosaic of hundreds of wonderful bits of color. It is an adaptation of antique Russian church decorations."

Gorgeous Blues, Crimsons, Yellows and Greens, as Beautiful as Enamel, in This New Decorative Art Work.

An enormous tiled oven, with a comfortable bench at the top on which they climb to get warm—all present a very riot of joyous color naïve design.

"The color seems to have actually run outside. For you will find the garden gates and wooden stands, the coaches, sledges, boats, carts and even farming implements gaily painted, "all during the long months of their bitterly cold winters, the peasants sit around the great oven, or on top of it, the women spinning, weaving, embroiling, the men creating necessary furniture and rioting in color and design. They use very vivid colors, like the Austrians, but they pack them close. A lot of colors placed in just a position to one another in an inset design, that presents from a distance just a mass of bright color. You see these two sketches" and she brought forth one.

The Bridal Chant

"Here is a reproduction of a bridal chest or 'scryni.' They are so beautiful. Every young girl has a chest in which she begins storing those wonderful embroidered towels and 'chirinkas'—storing up the most exquisite things for the day when she will be a bride. There is such a variety of them. Some chests flat on the floor, others with low legs, and still others which seem not at all like chests, so high is their pedestal like support. They all differ in color and line. Some in violently contrasting colors, strong orange, vermilion, and indigo, with squares of flaring white, and sapphire blue, a great sprawling ornament, rich and voluptuous in its swing. Others softer in outline and color of mellow golden, with over panting in line of flat scarlet and faded beautiful blue. And soma chests of daring blue with narrow panels of dark, copper red splashed over with a spotted vermilion design, broken with lines and checks of white. "The garden gates too, are particularly jolly, and are bound to become popular here In America. One that I saw was very fetching. It was a wooden entrance gate, just an archway covered with geometrical figures, circular designs in crude, strong color—the whole sheltered from the weather by a pointed cap roof of wall set shingles. A great deal of all this is already being taken up by Americans. Paul Poiret *(Clothing Designer 1879-1944)* and the Austrians with their futurist and modernist hangings and stuffs perhaps paved the way. And now come these things."

The New Spirit

Weber is of the new school of art, which is called by decorative workers, the Modernist, as all-embracing of the new spirit of strong color. "Most artists are following the new school," she explained. "I believe it marks growth, just as everything changes in the course of its progress. Time was, when a painter jugged his subject into a dark, gloomy corner of deep shadows and dabbed the dullest browns and blacks and murky grays and greens upon his canvas. Today, a new spirit is pervading everything. Dress is Influenced by it, interior decoration, upholsteries, hangings, furniture, painting and decorative art. Instead of seeking shadows, we are beginning to drag everything forth into the bright joyous sunshine and to see it all in glad colors. We are getting away from narrow, useless, binding conventions, from the suppression of individuality. It is revolutionizing, yes; but so is all freedom attained through revolution."

"THE POST-STAR," GLENS FALLS, N. Y.,
FRIDAY, OCTOBER 17, 1952

Mrs. Furlong Displaying Art Locally
Professional Artist Will Reside in City; Exhibit at Library

By JOSEPH J. DODGE

A new one-man show of colorful and decorative oil paintings has just opened at Crandall Library. The paintings are landscapes and still-life by Mrs. Weber Furlong, for 31 years she has been a summer resident of Bolton Landing and starting next month a winter resident of Glens Falls. This exhibition is by way of an Introduction of Mrs. Furlong to her new home and of the people of Glens Falls to a prominent professional artist.

Mrs. Furlong will establish a studio at 25 Ridge Street. This studio will be open in the afternoons after Nov. 1 to anyone interested in making use of her vast experience, enthusiasm, and facilities for painting.
She hopes to work with and give individual assistance to adults, either beginners or more experienced amateurs, who wish to "Discover them-selves through painting."

Born in St. Louis

Weber Furlong was born in St. Louis, as was her husband, Thomas Furlong, and she studied painting

99

under William Chase, Emile Carlson, Max Weber, and her husband — all of whom are very famous artists and teachers. Chase was probably the most highly regarded and most popular and successful painter in America about 50 years ago. Max Weber, who is still living, is one of the finest painters in America today, represented in practically every museum, and incidentally was the first person to bring pictures by Cézanne to America.

Thomas Furlong

Thomas Furlong was artist-in-residence at Champlain College until he died early this year. For 13 years, he was special artist for the Bethlehem Steel Corporation and had previously taught at Hunter College and New York University. For several years, he was co-director of the Furlong-Nicolaides School at 3 Washington Square in New York, which had a very high reputation at the time! Dorothy Dehner, whose paintings will be on view here next month, was one of their students.

Visited Mexico

Mrs. Furlong, who signs her paintings simply Weber visited Mexico for several years around 1910, before it was discovered by so many artists and tourists. Her paintings done there were exhibited in St. Louis and other places so that her reputation as a serious and competent artist goes back for at least 40 years. She married Thomas Furlong and settled In New York City in 1916.

Since then, besides her painting, she has acted as executive secretary of the famed Art Students League for seven years and later was secretary of the Furlong-Nicolaides School, with the result that she has a great knowledge of art schools and teaching methods and a personal acquaintance with hundreds of prominent artists.

She and her husband bought a farm in the hills above Bolton Landing, near the present golf course, in 1921 and have spent their summers there ever since. The property is known as Golden Heart Farm and is well-known in art circles because of the many artists and writers who have visited and worked there. It is full of fascinating objects of all sorts collected by the Furlongs over the years; many of which will be moved to her Ridge Street studio to be used as subjects for still lives.

Mrs. Furlong believes that such lovely old things have a life of their own and she succeeds in expressing that animation in her paintings.

TO EXHIBIT WORK
AT BOLTON BANK

BOLTON LANDING. —

A group of still-life and landscapes by Weber Furlong will be exhibited in the lobby of the Bolton Landing branch of the First National Bank of Glens Falls during banking hours next week. Weber Furlong, Mrs. Thomas Furlong in private life, studied with Werpel, William Chase, Emil Carlsen, Max Weber, and Thomas Furlong. For seven years she was executive secretary of the Art Students League of New York City. She was secretary of The Furlong-Nicolaides School, Washington Square, New York. Recently she assisted her late husband, the artist in-residence at Champlain College, Pittsburgh, through numerous exhibitions from the Metropolitan and the Modern museums; lectures and creating the North Country artists' annual exhibition at Pittsburgh. She is now interested in such a movement in Bolton Landing. Her current exhibition is at her home, Golden Heart.

Bolton Bank Shows
Area Artists Work

During the Holiday Season, the Bolton Bank is happy to present the first group exhibit of the work of area artists. Two new exhibitors are included, their work bringing added vitality and diversity to the show. They are Hanna Bauer, who has been drawing and painting in oils for some years and has worked in fashion designing, and Olga Ronning. Mrs. Ronning was formerly a head textile designer for the famous Cheney Bothers Mills at Manchester, Connecticut. Since her marriage she is living near Bolton and is still associated with Cheney Bros. She studied at the National Academy, New York School of Design, and at N. Y. U. and Columbia University.

New work by artists who have previously shown at the Bank include:

"Concha on a Raft" by *Weber Furlong,* "Grand Mother" by Rose Dagles, "Pigeon Cove" by Helen Hamilton and "Our Lady of New York Harbor" by Elsa Steinback.

The Bank presents this show primarily for the enjoyment of all and the stimulation of interest in creative art which should by no means be thought necessarily limited to large cities where museums, galleries and art schools are chiefly located. The understanding and appreciation of any creative art is a valuable addition to daily life for it can bring a new measure of beauty, or perception, in a world faced with so many problems.

Historical Impact and Modern Women

I only recently realized that Golden Heart Farm may have been one of the earliest art colonies in the United States during the High Modernist movement, a period in art history that was to bring much credit to American art and to our artists. Was Golden Heart Farm one of the first artist in-residence programs in the United States that focused on modernism and on self-awareness?

With her early arrival to the Modernist movement in Paris during the 1890s, she witnessed the transition of great importance. That, with her incredible life in New York City before 1900, makes Wilhelmina Weber the innovative early American woman modernist, pre-dating the high modernist movement in America by two decades.

Wilhelmina Weber was indeed ahead of her time and she had been a part of the art community for so long that I am sure she understood this. Life was difficult for a young woman artist before 1900, and as modernism flourished, the world was struggling to accept much change. It was in the arts where women like this were at a disadvantage, as were women everywhere. It was difficult for any young woman in the 1890s. Many survived from their wealthy families, and others worked hard to maintain the life they loved so much. Hers was the life of painting and free expression. We are fortunate to have the works and life of Wilhelmina Weber in the paintings and art she left behind. Wilhelmina Weber belonged to a unique period for early American women artists, a period she richly influenced during her time in New York City and at Golden Heart Farm. Modern women would become largely more influential within the early American Modern Art community as the movement drew near its end in 1950. Modern women artists flourished throughout the latter half of the twentieth century.

How did we arrive here? First, through the Archives of American Art at the Smithsonian Institute when the archives first came on-line, I contacted them about the Furlong and Weber letters that I saved from Golden Heart. They expressed a real interest in the Wilhelmina Weber Furlong and Thomas Furlong letters. What I initially found in the Smithsonian archives was a series of oral history interviews with Dorothy Dehner, (1965 Oct.-1966 Dec, Archives of American Art, Smithsonian Institution). This defining discovery started the interest in a project of this nature, to document the lives of two people I had never met and a place I had never been.

Second, my retiring in 2010 and returning home allowed me the time to do more research for the substantial project, which had only been a dream before this point in my life. It had always been my intention to do something with the collection of paintings and writings. At this point, I created the Weber Furlong Collection to reintroduce Wilhelmina Weber to the world. Soon after setting up the Weber Furlong website, I was fortunate to have been contacted by Joseph Dodge, the son of Jerry Dodge mentioned earlier.

During the spring of 2011, it was through fate that I came to meet Mona Blocker Garcia, herself an international American woman and founder of the International Woman's Foundation in Marfa, Texas. Marfa was the residence of Donald Judd, who years ago, I had the pleasure of meeting while in school near Marfa. The International Woman's Foundation owns and maintains Building 98, which houses the historic World War II German POW murals at Ft. D. A. Russell, a US Army Cavalry post formerly known as Camp Marfa. German artists Hans Jurgen Press and Robert Hampel painted the murals. Both were imprisoned alongside members of Rommel's élite North Africa Korps.

In Marfa, I set out on the intricate and costly task of photographing and cataloguing the collection, for the first time ever. I had already contacted the David Smith Foundation in New York, and the Hyde Collection in Glens Falls, both of which responded with excitement and enthusiasm, for this significant project. Erin Coe, the current Chief Curator at the Hyde, has been a vital asset to the Weber Furlong Project as it has evolved to the present day. As the person responsible for the now very prestigious museum collections, Erin has increased the number of Weber Furlong paintings at the museum to include "Jazz" a magnificent still-life she allowed us to view during the filming of the documentary in Glens Falls and Bolton Landing. In all, there are four Weber Furlong paintings and one Thomas Furlong in the Hyde Museum's collection.

The Weber Furlong Exhibition is a labor of love aimed at telling the story of Wilhelmina Weber and displaying her astonishing art. All of us involved with the project would like the world to appreciate her art and understand the historical significance of Golden Heart Farm. Had she not been so prolific with her art, none of this would be happening today. Her hard work has made everything fall into place. Her true life's story spans three continents, contains romance, excitement, love, achievement, and adventure! Without the photographic record and personal materials in the estate of Wilhelmina Weber, we may have been unable to piece together the life of the woman we now know as Wilhelmina Weber Furlong.

Thanks to Bernard Weber III, my father, and my mother Mitzi, we have access to her art and personal belongings for study. The close bond to his great-aunt led me to compile this story on the life of Wilhelmina Weber and her husband the artist Thomas Furlong before it becomes lost to time.

Her cards and letters to my parents reveal much about the woman Wilhelmina Weber. A 1957 note explains some of her life in Glens Falls:

"I paint from 5:00 AM to 10:00 AM. I enjoy painting more than anything in my life! I only have a few hours to paint; I wish I could paint all day."

"There are always young people in and out of the studio it seems to me that youth has such a tough time now - no leisure - no time to examine themselves - to think - moving like a cog in a wheel. I have a little sign in the work studio.

No Contemplation

No Imitation

No Limitation (Spiritual)

No Expectations (Material)

This will produce a happy person."

"Paint as you feel, express yourself"

As a child, I discovered the following tucked away in the old black briefcase, with the Weber and the Furlong papers. It is a poem or sonnet she had typewritten on a sheet of paper with no credited author:

The May

"May time is a flower time, color brown and gay,
Never a field in funereal in the month of May.
Hepaticas and yellow-bells,
Lady –slippers, daffodils,
Forget-me-not's and berry-vines,
Calliopes and columbines.

Never a field so miserly hoards its crop of hay,
As not to give the flowers room in the month of May.
Seed and sun sonatas in all the gardens play,
Color tinkles from the earth in the month of May.
Lilacs lavenderly blow,
Tulips chastely stand a-row,
Hyacinths and jonquils nod
Out of newly bedded sod.

Never a spot so impiously bare as not to pray
For adventitious flowers- in the month of May.
May time brings to life again every orchard Fay,
Flower-full and powerful, in the month of May
Apple-trees turn twisted limbs

Into mystical white hymns,

Cherry-tree is flaked with rose,

Plum-tree lyrically goes.

Never a tiny butterfly known to orchard Fay

But wears a mask of petals − in the month of May.

Deep within the forest dark where the late snows lay,

Flowers venture bravely in the month of May.

Arbutus and anemones,

Violets and valley-lilies,

Wild-fruit blossoms tremble high,

Dogwood clusters from the fly

Never a leafy forest, merely green, so gay

As wild flower forest in the month of May

May time is a flower time, color brown and gay,

Never a field funereal in the month of May.

Farm and field and furrow,

Dell and brake and burrow,

Forest, hill, and wild wayside,

Chorical and flower eyed.

Never a country carnival on a gala day,

Half so gay as countryside in the month of May."

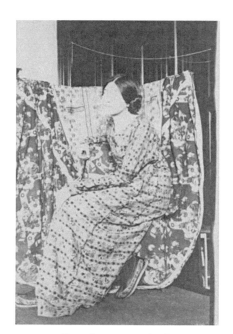

Study, ca. 1913

ca. 1907

(Weber Furlong Exhibit Poster) Photo, Paris, ca. 1898
Family Quote:
"We all like this one of you so much it is you, to the life"

Exhibit Retrospective

The Wilhelmina Weber Furlong project is an ongoing and cumbersome task. In an effort to preserve the collection and its contents, every detail demands close attention. The costly process of conservation must begin now that the collection out for public viewing. The objective is to analyze the collection, to preserve its contents, and define an artist of important stature in the art community then and now. Building the chronology takes on great importance so we can have an effective timeline of events. None of the artwork was initially viewable since they had been stored without frames or stretchers for fifty years. Fortunately, they were in airtight sealed containers. Additionally, many aspects about the life of the artist reveal itself in the letters and writings of this substantial collection.

The presentation and curation of the exhibit is a detailed process requiring graphic design and documentation to give the public an opportunity to understand the event and its importance. To assist the curation project a High definition documentary format became the medium to present the detailed process from start to finish. Storylines compiled the interview and filming process. Oral history interviews tell the story from a firsthand perspective. Establishing contacts in the local community of Glens Falls, Saratoga Springs, and Bolton Landing became an easy task. Because Wilhelmina Weber was so well known, the project took on a life of its own. The children of her closest friends contacted the exhibit through our website. Once people became aware of the project, more contact with people who had known Wilhelmina occurred rapidly. Several people had childhood memories of her which they recalled joyfully. The story line simply created itself through the lives of the people she touched. Local museums had her paintings on display since the early 1960s.

The Weber Furlong Foundation has been created to span in historical and chronological order the periods and artistic styles known to us from today's perspective. We feel the list below represents Wilhelmina Weber's formal works, as seen today from a wide range of understanding. Some of the influences are rather bold and others show only a hint. Both cultural and social expressions are evident in her body of work painted between 1890 and 1962.

Modernism

Expressionism

Abstract Expressionism

Post Impressionism

Fauvism

Cubism

Artists that would follow Wilhelmina Weber also grew to earn their place in American Art History. The art styles would shift dramatically from the styles Wilhelmina Weber came to know and love in the 1890's. Her bold imagery has survived for further study since the journey has only just begun to analyze her place as a significant contributor to the art world in America.

One can get lost while viewing her paintings, and seeing something different every time, as I have for forty-one years. Even more amazing is the feeling I get when some-one points out something I never noticed after so many years of observations. After the point in time of Wilhelmina Weber and on into the post-modern period, women had much stronger possibilities to become highly visible. They would become even more outspoken, even challenging in the art communities.

Modernism reveals itself in the works of art on display. We see the modern and yet impressionistic quality of the work which at times displays classic cubism. Her prolific oils on canvas and ornate watercolors show rich colors and the emotion of the artist. Abstract and impressionistic, still-life and landscape, and a salvaged mural all are treasures once lost to public viewing. We see the artistic cultural movement at its height, and at a time of great significance. Yet, we understand the simplicity; the short-lived movement so desperately desired. Would things change? Would the world enrich itself in one's daily life? In addition, could the movement ever recover from the loss of two great wars, and a great depression? The sad reality was no. The artistic trend ended almost as quickly as it had begun, in a whirling vortex of modern enlightenment, and progressive change.

Life at Golden Heart Farm was the much-loved life of enlightenment, clarification, and creativity, a modern yet basic life where needs were kept primitive and thought was allowed to progress forward. After World War I, Wilhelmina Weber began to experience the ascent into modernism as a viewpoint in the arts, and by 1960, she had seen its demise. Consequently, she was unable to survive as an artist past the progressive and political realities of the time. At age 83 and near blind, she lived long enough to see her movement arrive and eventually shift to the postmodernism of America, a movement she had richly influenced during her early days at Golden Heart Farm. Modern women would come to have the benefit of the attention they deserved after many years of struggles to achieve creative and artistic independence. This struggle has continued into our century and we understand it was in the arts that women like Wilhelmina Weber made much progress to that freedom.

Found among her letters was Aunt Wilhelmina (Minnie's) Weber's prayer book, "The Book of Common Prayer" for the Episcopal Church, dated 1893. Inside were pressed flowers and two Tiny Tot Tales, "Meddlesome Molly the Bad Little Dolly" by Martha Hart and several old photographs of her father. In Bolton Landing, she attended the Episcopal Church of St. Sacrament. In 1954, across from the Episcopal Church, artists from a fifty-mile area of the Bolton Landing home of Roy B. Anderson used the grounds for a local exhibition of art, the second annual outdoor Bolton Landing art exhibition for which Mrs. Weber Furlong of Bolton Landing was listed as a contact.

Her darkly stained Victorian easel stands out, along with her original paintbrushes and an old paint box my father gave her in 1948, complete with dried-up paint my mother somehow managed to save. Also of interest are an old, rather small glass Victorian oil lamp, and an interesting bootlace pick. These are but a few of the things displayed at the exhibition for insight into the life and times of Wilhelmina Weber.

The Wilhelmina Weber Estate is relatively large, and contains enough items to outfit a small house. Her mother's dramatic flow blue china along with the pitchers and bowls she painted in still-life are paramount among her family's belongings. This china was described in social columns at the time of her regional exhibitions. There are several dozen art, and fine arts magazines that the Estate managed to save, dating from 1850 to 1950, as well as several hundred stereoscopic cards and viewers. Postcards and family photographs offer insight into the life of the artist. I also found the Farmer's Almanac from 1834 and 1919 tucked inside one of her books.

The Weber Furlong Collection includes a metal engraving with "Faith Whitney" written on the back, and we think it is noteworthy. The Furlongs used it for a Champlain College greeting card they produced. The engraving featured alongside an old ink roller catches one's eye. The Furlongs had a small artist in residence cottage on campus for several years. From 1946 to 1952, Champlain College was used as an emergency institution at the home of the 26th Infantry. Created for WWII veterans who returned home to take advantage of the GI Bill, the college served many. Thomas Furlong was a founding faculty member at the institution.

Metal Engraving from Champlain College
Plattsburg, New York, Ca 1946

In 1926, the Furlongs mass-produced the "Woman at the Well," from a detailed 16th century woodblock in perfect condition. We donated one of these prints to the Bolton Landing Historical Society Museum in 2012 following the visit for the "In Search of Weber" documentary project. The Bolton Landing Museum permanently displays two works by Wilhelmina Weber Furlong.

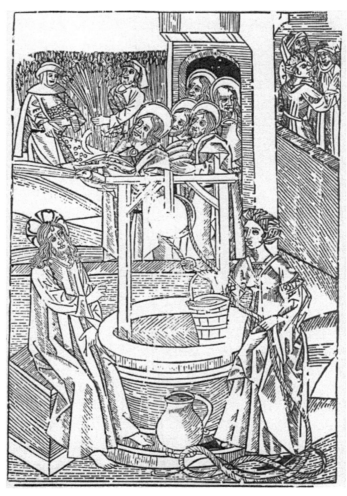

"The Woman at the Well," reproduced 1926

Also featured in the collection is an etching by Kenneth Hayes Miller (1876-1952), who taught at the Art Students League from 1911 to 1951. Kenneth Miller was a close friend of Thomas and Wilhelmina while in Greenwich Village. The friendship came to an abrupt end after Miller's conservative viewpoints on traditional old masters art resulting in a division at the Art Students League over Weber's approach to modernism as part of the League's program.

Wilhelmina Weber's role at the Art Students League was one of importance. She had been in this position for many years. She was an active woman in the New York Art community because of this prominent position at the League. The role of Executive Secretary and the League's Treasurer was one she did not take lightly. She did take an interest in the students and in the teachers with which the students were exposed. This passionate interest ultimately led to this controversial rift. This would occur well into her tenure at the Art Students League as a devoted administrator and member. She obviously felt compelled to promote modernism as a serious form of artistic expression at a time when the movement had experienced great success in America.

Weber and Thomas had become friends with Willem De Konning after meeting him through John Graham at the 3 Washington square studio address in 1929. By 1939, she felt he was an artist of significant importance to the Modern Art movement. She tried to hire him as an instructor at the Art Students League. Unfortunately, Kenneth Miller did not agree with Wilhelmina Weber. For several years the two artists held opposing sides to the direction of the Leagues curriculum and staff. At times, it was intolerable to Wilhelmina Weber who had devoted her life to the Art Students League. One can easily understand professional and differing viewpoints and the controversy they cause often to the point of the devastation of an individual or a career. It was Professor James Kettlewell, who remembers it was this rift of viewpoints, which led Wilhelmina Weber to resign from her position at the Art Students League. This setback did not slow her down, however it did mean the couple would face times that were more difficult. After the death of Thomas Furlong in 1952, Wilhelmina Weber perused her own work as an artist. She provided for herself quite well as woman artist during these years.

The Artist Morgan Dennis (1892-1960) had met the Furlongs and had given them one of the production drawings from 'Himself and Burlap" on TV, an early cartoon production seen on television.

Max Weber the Modern Artist was communicating with Wilhelmina Weber. Found in her notes this handmade greeting card sent to her inscribed by Max along with an exhibition booklet from a Max Weber show with several doodles he inscribed to Weber. Max and Wilhelmina had met years' earlier in Paris and Wilhelmina spoke of him affectionately as one of her dearest lifelong friends.

Max Weber, 1930

Kenneth Hayes Miller

Godey's Lady's book

Wilhelmina's mother Magdelina (Maggie) saved copies of this pre-Civil War "Godey's Lady's Book", from January through December 1851. They likely had come from her family's general store in St. Louis. Godey's was a pictorial literary magazine, featuring American writers and artists. Louis A. Godey and Mrs. S. J. Hale, Editors published it in Philadelphia. It promoted free enterprise through advertising. Wilhelmina and her mother were quite close. She held on to many of her mother's belongings, all on display in the exhibit. Wilhelmina spent much of her childhood with her grandparents at their general store. They always had fabulous birthday and Halloween costumes made for their granddaughter.

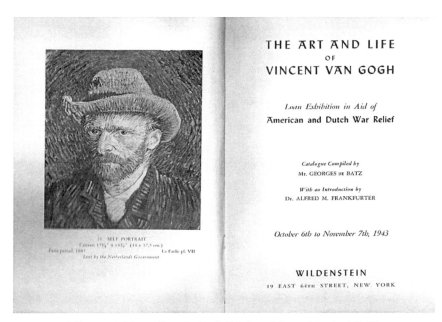

Vincent Van Gogh Exhibition New York 1943

We know that Wilhelmina Weber attended a Vincent Van Gogh exhibition in November of 1943. The event was in New York City for war relief. The program above is included in the exhibit. Prior to World War II, life was very difficult for Wilhelmina Weber and her husband. They barely made ends meet, and the stock market crash wiped out a good portion of her brother's fortune. They were able to survive by their combined professional talents and income from the retreat at Golden Heart Farm. Therefore, by the time this Vincent Van Gogh war relief event occurred, things were looking better for them. Participation in the war effort was common in the communities of New York City and Glens Falls. This exhibition marked the turning point for Allied forces in Europe, and many turned their attention to using their skills to help relieve the despair most Europeans were experiencing.

Wilhelmina Weber was actively painting during this period and participating in cultural events in New York City at the Art Students League and the Whitney Studio Club from 1913 and on to the 1940s. The couple maintained social contacts in New York all through their lives.

Like most women of her time, she would focus her efforts on assisting her husband. She gave up promoting her work almost entirely to assist Thomas Furlong in his pursuit of success as an artist in New York City. This effort to support Thomas set her back, as she helped him achieve his goals, a point discovered by her friend and art historian James Kettlewell who recalled this from a conversation with her shortly after they had met. By the time she emerged, the movement shifted to larger works that became more abstract. One must also understand Thomas Furlong to understand Wilhelmina Weber. The mutual love the couple had throughout their life is paramount to understanding the couple. The couple would never lose sight of the love they shared for each other.

Wilhelmina Weber, ca. 1915

Wilhelmina Weber at Golden Heart, 1925

Wilhelmina Weber, Golden Heart Gallery Hall, ca. 1955

Note the historic "Portrait of Wilhelmina"

By Thomas Furlong in the background featured at the Hyde
Collection Museum

Glens Falls, ca. 1957

Glens Falls, ca. 1957

Thomas Furlong and the Mexican Revolution

To define the role of Mr. Thomas Furlong and Miss Wilhelmina Weber in Mexican history, we turn to Thomas's business efforts with his father. Specifically, they came to be close allies to President Porfirio Diaz. By fate, Thomas and Wilhelmina had come to meet in Mexico City. The two shared a common heritage and unusual common interests. Both were from St. Louis and both were interpreters and New York artists. Both were educated, well spoken, and experienced in the ways of the world. Moreover, they were both a long way from home. The journey to this part of the world was a long and difficult one in the early 1900s.

What an amazing twist of providence, this chance meeting of two very similar people in the same place and time, serving the same cause. Was it Thomas and Wilhelmina's strong will that led them to meet in such a remote region of the world? These were dangerous times for a country in turmoil. In reality, was political mayhem what actually allowed them to meet?

One might conclude that all events that led to their meeting make a strong case for the predetermined nature of peoples' lives. The two shared a love of art, but also the understanding that all must make a living, always moving towards independence and self-awareness. It was on this journey that Thomas and Wilhelmina's paths crossed during their work with President Diaz in Mexico City. The account is real and the events a matter of history.

After they met, their lives together continued to grow, first as friends, then as lovers, and finally as partners in life and professional colleagues in the art community of New York. We have a detailed account of much of their life together and of their adventure.

Spring, 1911

Pictured here are Mr. Thomas Furlong and Miss Wilhelmina Weber in Mexico, in the spring of 1911. In the photo are

Miss K. B. Ledford, and Mrs. B.C. Hill, well-dressed and well-protected. The somewhat large group of people seems to be enjoying themselves, as if there was not a worry in the world. However, these were not safe times to be in remote Mexico!

Thomas Furlong was in Mexico from 1911 to 1912, and the nature of his work was of great importance to the President of Mexico. Both Thomas and his father had been gathering intelligence for President Diaz. His father was an acclaimed secret agent during the American Civil War, and had been among the Union's first in service. He worked for the Pennsylvania Railroad, Missouri Pacific Railroad, police agencies and as the Police Chief of Oil City, Pennsylvania. He formed the Furlong's Secret Service Company, established in 1880, after a long and very successful career rounding up murderous outlaws and generally bad characters. On July 26, 1889, he was slated to become Chief of the U.S. Secret Service, one of Jay Gould's most energetic detectives. He was described in the "World Newspaper" of New York as one who could do the dirty work required by the good railroad king. (Vol. XXX, No. 10,902).

During the dangerous height of the Madero Revolution, Thomas Furlong worked with his father for the Mexican authorities, one of the most interesting adventures of his career. This extraordinary time 1911-1912 in Mexico City concluded with their logistical plan for the President's successful exit out of Mexico to safe a haven in Europe, with his vast interests intact. Porfirio Diaz would pass away in Paris, France in 1915. Thomas and his father associated themselves with the Mexican government through Enrique Clay Creel (1854-1931). Theirs was a lengthy relationship. Creel was a very powerful Mexican businessman, politician, and Mexican-American War veteran. At that time, 1910 to 1911, he was the Minister of Foreign Affairs, after serving as Governor of Chihuahua, Mexico, from 1907 to 1910. He was a banker, industrialist, served as the Ambassador of Mexico to the United States in 1909, and was involved in international trade. With the government's assistance, the father-and-son team of this family-run business success-fully tracked down and captured a network of dissident spies and revolutionaries plotting against the Diaz Family. The elder Furlong had been working for the Mexican government between 1905 and 1906, when he had stopped an earlier armed force of insurgents fighting against the authority of the Madero Presidency, with gun battles and secret spy operations carefully thought out and organized by the Furlong Secret Service Agency. The pri-vate agency put their vast Civil War experience to work for the Mexican government for a total of seven years. Their later intelligence efforts were carefully coordinated from St. Louis. The Furlong agency apprehended revolutionary ex-iles in the United States and provided intelligence reports for the Mexican government. This all occurred before the creation of the various American state department agencies, as we know them today. They would be in ser-vice to Vice Presidents José María, Pino Suárez, and Ramón Corral. The Furlongs would report to the U.S. Department of State, and were assisted while in Mexico by the young Miss Wilhelmina Weber. The U.S. Department of State very closely monitored these activities. Wilhelmina Weber had U.S. embassy friends in Mexico and Venezuela, and assisted Thomas Furlong the interpreter during the final years of the Madero reign. This had gone on for many years beginning in 1906. She was in a rather difficult situation. However, the situation for her was not in her control. She was simply an interpreter and teacher with tremendous multilingual communication skills who had earned a great deal of trust within the personal lives of the Diaz family.

It was during the beginnings of this amazing international spy account that the Furlongs had come to meet Miss Wilhelmina Weber. She had been serving the first family of Mexico, assisting in personal family matters through translating, and teaching French to Mexican royalty and their children. They were all very loyal to the Diaz family during this interesting and controversial time. These circumstances were very early in the development of the American government's intelligence activities, and the two participated as interpreters for several years. This was a crucial and defining moment for the couple at that point in their life when they had come to meet. The couple had led an adventurous life in Mexico. To his families displeasure Wilhelmina Weber would pull Thomas Furlong from the family business to promote his career as an artist upon their return to Manhattan where she opened a studio and art gallery.

Wilhelmina Weber 1910

Thomas Furlong

Thomas Furlong painting one of many portraits of
Wilhelmina Weber in the Studio at
3 Washington Square, NYC, 1914

Thomas ("Tomas") Furlong 1886-1952, St. Louis

Thomas ("Tomas") Furlong, born on February 28, 1886, in St. Louis, Missouri, of Scotch-Irish and German descent, was "Professor Furlong" to his friends and colleagues at the School of Design and Liberal Arts, 212 West 59th Street, New York. Both Thomas and Wilhelmina taught at Champlain College in Plattsburg, New York. His first significant work was "Portrait of Wilhelmina Weber," in the spring of 1913, and "The Juggler," in the private collection of Dr. Gustav Lippman, St. Louis. "Portrait of Miss Wilhelmina Weber," painted after the two had met in Mexico became a showpiece for Thomas Furlong. The young artist, pictured in his studio above, shows a comfortably well-groomed man, standing out with style. Wilhelmina abundantly loved this young man. At the time of this photo, he taught at New York University and led a prominent life at an important time in American art history. In his prominent Washington Square studio, the outside world remains hidden from view.

Starting in 1913, Thomas was a successful illustrator and poster designer for "Vogue," "Vanity Fair," "Country Life," "Town and Country," and "Spur" magazines. That same year, he designed and executed the first modern stage set ever shown in New York, at Proctor's Fifth Avenue Theater.

Proctor's Fifth Avenue Theater was of historical significance to New York, as it was here that "The Pirates of Penzance" by Gilbert and Sullivan premiered in 1879. It later became the home of common bill vaudeville acts.

In addition, in 1913 Thomas Furlong designed a large decorative screen for the John Kuppenheimer home in Chicago.

After graduating from college in 1909 with a B.S. degree from Washington University in St. Louis, Thomas Furlong studied at the St. Louis Art School under Wuerpel, a pupil of Whistler. In 1909, he had a fellowship under John Vanderpoel Lewis at Lewis School in St. Louis. He then studied at the Art Students League in the summer of 1909, and went on to gain a competitive scholarship for the following year under F. Luis Mora and Frank Vincent Bridgman DuMond.

Thomas lived in Mexico from 1911 to 1912 as an interpreter between his father and Porfirio Diaz and Enrique C. Creel during the Madero Revolution of 1911. After meeting Wilhelmina Weber, he would return to New York where he drew for "Vogue" magazine.

In 1914, Thomas Furlong served during World War I as one of the executives of Postal Censorship, 641 Washington Street, New York in the capacity of (DAC) Direct Action Committee. In February of 1919, following the Armistice, he resigned to enter professional life again as a painter, three months after the treaty was signed on November 11, 1918.

In 1916, Thomas Furlong studied portrait painting with Robert Henry. In 1919, he studied life painting and composition with Kenneth Hayes Miller, followed by a development period of figure painting and composition, under Max Weber (1921-1922), along with his wife Wilhelmina Weber. In his own words, "my instructors were Kenneth Hayes Miller and Max Weber especially."

He continued his studies and worked at the Art Students League, in 1921, 1922, 1923, and 1925, not continuously, but as often as outside commissions permitted. He became a Board of Control member and Treasurer in 1921. In 1922, the Art Students League offered a teaching position to Thomas Furlong; however, he declined to remain on the Executive Board of Control and as the Treasurer. He would pursue business ventures within the community he served.

As an Executive Board Member of the Art Students League, Thomas Furlong had a prominent place in the art community he represented. This opened many doors for him, which could have been his primary reason for declining the teaching position at the League. In his curriculum vitae, he wrote that he preferred to pursue the executive position in the community. The League was a beneficial affiliation indeed. It would be hard to determine if accepting the offer would have affected his prominence as an artist. Nearly all of the instructors at the League reached great heights in their careers because of the status they earned teaching at the most prominent art institution in America.

In 1920, Thomas taught drawing and design at Bronx Evening High School. He was Chairman of the Drawing Department. The New York Department of Education 500 Park Avenue issued his teaching license on Thursday, May 4, 1920 at 9:00 AM.

From 1921 to 1925, he taught life class, antique, and mural projects in the New York School of Applied Design for Women, where he reintroduced the Beaux-Arts Mural Project in the school in 1926 to 1927. He taught watercolor and costume sketch classes there, where the students would sketch their designs in watercolor.

Thomas Furlong began his work with church murals in 1925, by repairing and recreating large sections of an altarpiece in St. Cyprian's Chapel, New York City. He would create murals such as the altarpiece in the Church of St. Vincent de Paul in Brooklyn, New York. His work with church art, led to an extensive résumé. Professor Furlong was one of the most trusted church restoration artists in New York City. The Furlong exhibit contains numerous photographic records of the churches he was responsible for restoring.

He served for several years as a member of the Jury of the Beaux-Arts Institute, composed of professional mural painters who judged mural painting projects. He was a member and a trustee of the American Fine Arts Society.

In 1926, he would start the Nicolaides and Furlong Atelier, a prestigious New York school for the teaching of life decorations and murals. The class conducted at 3 Washington Square, at the Washington Square Park became a positive turning point in his career with his associations earned in the teaching project.

In 1927, he began lecturing at New York University on Form, its analysis through type solids, its synthesis through representation, and free-hand perspective. He would teach the NYU art Course and supervise the entire program. He then had the curriculum of his lectures and his drawings compiled into the textbook used at New York University.

From 1925 to 1927, he would exhibit in the Independent Society of Painters, Fifty-Ninth Street Artists at Anderson Galleries, Graphic Arts Exhibition at National Arts Club,

Montrose Gallery, 50th Anniversary Exhibition of Art Students League, and the Architectural League of New York.

In his Curriculum Vitae, we find his description of his work in New York:

> The concrete evidence of attainment in mural painting of Professor Furlong's work is listed below in his own words.

1. Two Polychrome Triptiches, painted on gold leaf over gesso. Designed and tooled, containing in all six panels; our Lady of Perpetual Help, St. Theresa, the Sacred Heart, St. Francis of Assisi, St. Anthony of Padua composing the side Altars in St. Brigid's Church, St. Nicholas Avenue and Linden Street, Brooklyn (commissioned by McGill and Hamlin) 1925.

2. Polychrome Triptiche on gold leaf over gesso consisting of four panels; St. Francis of Assisi (different from the above St. Francis), St. Bernadine and two panels containing coats of arms of the Saints and of their Cities together with all over design of polychrome Gothic Tracery (commissioned by McGill and Hamlin) 1926.

3. The design and actual execution full size of the first modern stage set for Proctor's Fifth Avenue Theater (done and installed 1913) commissioned by Modern Studio, 9 West 42nd St, New York, City.

4. Design execution of Polychrome Borders and repainting of two side altar pieces, The Adoration of Shepherds and the Ascension in the Church of St. Mary of the Lake, White Bear, Minnesota

(done for Mrs. Michael Gavin, 12 East 65th Street, New York City) 1927

In Projects:

1. Sanctuary of Saint Mary of the Lake, White Bear, Minnesota. Space 24ft by 28ft approximately, (commissioned by Mrs. Michael Gavin, 12 East 65th Street, New York City) 1927.
2. Decoration for space 14ft x 14ft in French Ballroom of Mrs. Oliver Gould Jennings, 328 Fifth Avenue, New York City 1927.

Thomas Furlong was quite successful with the designs he created for John Wanamaker, the brother of the founder of the first department store in Philadelphia, Wanamaker's department store. In 1913, Thomas began painting ornate furniture designs for Section 400 of the store. Then, from 1914 to 1915, he designed sets of painted furniture, and from 1916 to 1918, made their fabric designs. There are numerous letters to Thomas Furlong from the Wanamaker stores, with locations in Paris, Philadelphia, and New York. Several of his fabric examples are on display in the Weber Furlong Collection.

He was an active Mason throughout his life, as was his father. Thomas Furlong described at Champlain College, as not being a modern extremist within the Modern Art movement, was a meticulous painter. Additionally, his landscapes, described as "uncomplicated," tend to be impressionistic in nature. Articles reveal he painted outside at high noon to capture the full color and light of day. During his lifetime, he exhibited at the Albany Institute of Art and History, and the Metropolitan Museum of Art invited him to exhibit at their institution, which he quickly accepted. He taught at the Hartford Art School, Hunter College, and his work was held in many collections during his lifetime. During New Deal, he painted murals for the Federal Arts Project between 1935 and 1943. The artistic community of New York was heavily involved with federal assistance for the arts.

Chicago's Wrigley Clock Tower, ca. 1925-1935

Significant to Chicago, Illinois, is Furlong's watercolor of the Wrigley Building clock tower, painted for the grand mural commissioned by Mr. and Mr. Oliver Gould Jennings at the Bethlehem Steel Building in Chicago. Mr. Jennings, who later recruited Thomas to design his private residence on behalf of his wife, admired this watercolor. The mural project was of prime importance to the young artist and his beloved wife. He served as special artist for Bethlehem Steel for thirteen years, where he painted works representing the complete steel process, from mining to finished product. This association was a lasting influence, both personally and professionally.

Mural commissioned by Mr. and Mr. Oliver Gould Jennings at the Bethlehem Steel Building in Chicago.

The Furlongs eventually created designs and participated in event planning by Mrs. Jennings for many of their ballroom events in New York and at their private residence. Some held in conjunction with the Art Students League are documented with numerous letters and receipts, letters of payment, and some rather personal and friendly communications with the Jennings family are included. Some of the Furlong letters are noteworthy and of some significance as they pertain to the personal and professional lives of Mr. and Mrs. Jennings. Thomas Furlong created interior decorations for Mrs. Oliver Gould Jennings at their residence. Thomas Furlong was a very smart man, dapper and always well-groomed. This set well with the industrialist and business mogul. The accomplished and highly esteemed artist was respected in the art communities of New York, Minnesota, and Chicago. He was a well-spoken man and always had the respect of those he met.

Worthy of mention is that Thomas Furlong's mentor, Kenyon Cox at the Art Students League became very well-known in Chicago for the 1893 Murals at the Columbian Exposition. Mr. Cox remained available as a reference to his friend and colleague Thomas Furlong.

Thomas Furlong's Bethlehem Steel building murals in Chicago, also on display, stand as a prime example of his artistic abilities. Almost lost to art historians, we are very fortunate to have several of them available to study further.

A collection of Fairfield, Connecticut letters includes those from Mary Burr Jennings, the grandmother of Mr. Jennings, who had purchased several paintings from the Furlongs at the 3 Washington Square Studio in New York, around July of 1929. The sale included paintings from both Thomas Furlong and Wilhelmina Weber. The letters concern their packaging, shipping, insurance, and delivery to a farm in Fairfield. Both parties had mentioned Golden Heart Farm in their letters that summer and life in New York City. Mary Jennings had returned from abroad that month, and upon her return to New York, she had been telephoned by Thomas Furlong to discuss the business arrangements. The telephone number was jotted down as "eight eighty-two in Fairfield" in one of his notes

Thomas Furlong married Wilhelmina Weber in 1916. On June 3, he wrote a letter home to tell his mother and sister that he and Weber preferred to have a simple civil ceremony. The Furlong family was supportive of his decision, and they were pleased about the forthcoming marriage. The couple had known each other for about three years finding love in Old Mexico. His sister, Ella D. Dawson, who at that time was the Secretary-Treasurer of the Furlong Secret Service Agency, oddly instructed Thomas Furlong to save the marriage certificate.

Thomas Furlong was a very talented muralist and painter who enjoyed his New York City life for many reasons. Like his wife after they acquired Golden Heart 1921, he would often find work projects that would afford him the opportunity to revisit the city at differing or alternating times with his wife. He would remain very active, as time would allow, with the events and projects of the Art Students League following his distinguished teaching career. It would seem often the two swapped out time in New York City while the other remained at Golden Heart. As time progressed, both of his wife's parents would eventually move into the farmhouse at Golden Heart. It was there at home, that both mother and father would eventually pass. They were a very close family, and Thomas Furlong and Wilhelmina Weber cared for her parent's right up to the very end.

Thomas would spend time at Golden Heart while Wilhelmina Weber was busy at her studio in the village or working at the Art Students League. Several letters and doodled post cards reveal this was very much the case all the way through their life together.

Throughout the 1920s, after leaving New York City by train and making it to Albany, New York, they would catch the northbound ferry, Albany Daily Number 33, which departed at 7:15 AM and landed in Lake George at 9:45 AM.

The Horicon, a Steamer of the Lake George and Lake Champlain Steam Boat Company, would depart Lake George to Bolton Landing, with two stops in between, one at Trout Pavilion and the other at Pilot Knob, before arriving at Bolton Landing at 10:25 AM. Passenger fares ran between 60 and 90 cents. This transportation company maintained a fleet of six steamboats: The Vermont, Ticonderoga, Chateaugat, Horicon, Sagmore, and the Mihican. The Delaware and the Hudson River Railroad connected with the Lake George and Lake Champlain Steam Boat Company arrivals.

Thomas Furlong and Wilhelmina Weber seated in front of their beloved Golden Heart Farm. ca. 1939

Pictured here is August C. Weber (hat in lap), father of Wilhelmina Weber, on the deck of the Horicon on a summer trip to stay at Golden Heart in 1923.

Her father Mr. August C. Weber was a prominent St. Louis candy maker who had his very successful business in the heart of St. Louis. He and his new son-in-law Thomas Furlong became close friends. They spent a great deal of time together as a family, and Thomas formed very strong bonds with the Weber Family.

Magdelina Meyer Weber and August C. Weber, ca. 1923

For Wilhelmina and her esteemed guests, much of the romance of Golden Heart Farm was in getting there. The trip was then and still is today a wonderful and perfect journey for anyone wishing to see the lakes. Whether by water, rail, or automobile, the family would find a quaint and welcoming community. The region itself was full of rich colorful local history. Today as an art and cultural center, Bolton Landing and Glens Falls provide one a chance to go back to a simpler time, when the basics in life were close to the heart of some of America's greatest free thinkers and innovators of the day. Lake George is still a place where people go to escape the fast-paced life of the big city. In 1921, Wilhelmina Weber felt the same way about the community as we do today.

SCHOOL OF DESIGN AND LIBERAL ARTS
212 West 59th St., Phone Circle 1850

Life: Drawing; Painting; Composition
            Daily except Monday and Saturday   9:30-12:30
Design: Textile; Com. Illustration; Costume; Batik
            Tuesday, Wed. Thursday, Friday   10:00-4:00
Crafts: Bookbinding; Weaving; Pottery; Block Printing
            Monday, Tues., Wed., Thurs., Fri.   10:00-4:00
History: A Study of Human Development
            Wednesday and Friday   11:30-12:30
Literature; Original Composition; Study of Modern Drama
            Tuesday and Thursday   11:30-12:30
Applied Design: Wednesday   1:30- 5:30

M. A. Amsden, Weaving; E. Van Sweringen, Bookbinding
Thomas Furlong, Applied Design; A. E. Baggs; Pottery

Single or group courses special rates. Send for circular.
Irene Weir, Director.

Class Offerings, School of Design and Liberal Arts

This interesting note card gives insight into the student's choices at the New York School of Design and Liberal Arts, where Thomas Furlong taught the course of applied design from 1921 to 1925. The six-hour course covered Textiles, Composition, Illustration, Costume, and Batik, the Javanese form of wax-resistant cloth dyeing with traditional patterns.

A one-man Champlain College exhibition featured 36, paintings by Thomas Furlong. It was a group of 36 studies of light and color made in Martha's Vineyard. Professor Furlong opened a new art gallery at the college in Building 2 located between the Administration Building and Chamberland Hall. The inaugural exhibit was to announce the art schedule of painting and drawing, as well as classes in landscape conducted by Professor Furlong. In 1946, he also helped establish the Engineering Department at Champlain College as a founding faculty member.

1926 The Nicolaides and Furlong Atelier

The Nicolaides and Furlong Atelier was a school for the teaching of life decorations and painting. The class, conducted at the Furlong's prestigious NYU campus address of 3 Washington Square, at the Washington Square Park, immediately became a hit. Thomas Furlong partnered with Kimon Nicolaides (1891-1938) for this successful course, with the support of their close friend Rockwell Kent (1882-1971), the noted muralist and illustrator who illustrated the book Moby Dick and N by E. Weber was the secretary of the popular art school.

Kimon Nicolaides was a teacher at the Art Students League when he met Thomas Furlong in the early 1920s. The two worked together and decided to teach, so they formed the Nicolaides and Furlong Atelier. Both men were dedicated artists and teachers. This was, for all practical purposes, a business venture between them. The program became quite successful in 1926. Kimon would return to the League to teach after having been a student.

THOMAS FURLONG
KIMON NICOLAIDES
3 WASHINGTON SQUARE · NORTH
NEW YORK CITY

Thomas Furlong and Kimon Nicolaides Letterhead

For fifteen years, Wilhelmina Weber lived in Greenwich Village in New York intermittently between 1892 and 1906. With time out of New York City to study in St Louis and Paris, these were her defining years. Wilhelmina Weber then settled in New York permanently by 1913, for a second and final time after her return from Mexico. The Village prior to 1900 was a gathering place for artists and painters. Between 1892 and 1895, the young Wilhelmina, accompanied by her father, would meet her acclaimed teacher William Merritt Chase at the Tenth Street Studio Building. They would reside intermittently at the Hotel St. Stephan until the year 1906. The time was broken up with two periods in Paris and her following her teacher's schools. In his senior years, her father, A. C. Weber, stayed with them at the prestigious 3 Washington Square Park address. By 1921, her mother would always stay at the farm, as she preferred it there. The two popular New York City addresses we find in the archives are below:

(1913-1914) the Studio and Gallery at 122 E. 59th Street

(1914-1939) 3 Washington Square at the park

The Manhattan studio and storefront gallery of Wilhelmina Weber became quite popular in 1913 it was part of the birth of the modernist movement in America. The New York Tribune highlighted it a year after she had opened it.

This Agreement, MADE the first

day of October   in the year one thousand nine hundred and twenty-nine
between   Thomas Furlong and Wilhelmine Weber Furlong

part ies of the first part, hereinafter called the LESSOR and   Ernest Lawson

party of the second part, hereinafter caller the LESSEE,
That the LESSOR hereby demises and lets unto the LESSEE, and the LESSEE does hereby hire and take from
the LESSOR, all those certain rooms known as rear studio   apartment, on the first floor
of the Apartment House No. 3 Washington Square, North   and known as

for the term of one year
to commence October first   1929 and to end September 30 1930; to be occupied as a
private dwelling apartment by the LESSEE and his family only, consisting of   persons.
And the said LESSEE hereby covenants and agrees to pay unto the said LESSOR rental, in equal monthly
payments, in advance, on the first day of every month during said term as follows:

One hundred and thirty-five dollars ($135.00) on the 1st of each

month.

3 Washington Square Lease, 1929-1930

Thomas Furlong and Wilhelmina Weber's 3 Washington Square address was also the studio location of a close friend and upstairs neighbor, Edward Hopper (1882-1967). The New York realist painter and printmaker already had become quite successful. They had rented the studio from the artist Ernest Lawson (1873-1939) who the Furlongs had met at the 1913 Armory show, years earlier. Mr. Lawson was selling his paintings at Wilhelmina Weber's gallery on 122 E. 59th Street.

The couple maintained a very socially active lifestyle from this studio. They held events and taught art classes together from this sophisticated apartment house. Their many students would exhibit their work collectively in a group environment from here. Held on a regular basis, Thomas Furlong entertained his guests with his piano concertos. This was a popular social event where people gathered to promote their efforts.

147

Whitney Studio Club

In New York at this time, 1914 to 1928 Wilhelmina Weber attended the Whitney Studio Club exhibitions, which would eventually become the Whitney Museum of American Art. This was an important part of her life with Thomas Furlong. The couple had been dedicated to the modernist movement with great enthusiasm by this time. Their close friends, and contemporaries in art were also devoted to the Studio Club events and social gatherings. This social interaction was an effort to promote modernism and help Modern Artists from all over. The goal was acceptance in the art community as serious figures in an important movement.

The Whitney Studio Club played a vital role in the movement by supporting many American artists. This was also a vital venue for emerging artists in the modernist movement. Without the support of the Studio Club, many would not have been able to exhibit their work. This endeavor was something she felt was critical to her belief that the modernist was part of a formal and significant movement; a movement as an American woman she pioneered.

For many years, Wilhelmina Weber was involved with the preparation of Gallery events for the Studio Club, shortly before the interim Whitney Studio Galleries announcement in the fall of 1928 that the club had achieved its goal: bringing the Modernist movement to the forefront. The Whitney Museum Library currently displays a letter to Miss Wilhelmina Weber in their online archives concerning the payment of $565 dollars for the use of an Art Students League gallery for a traveling art show. The letter, dated May 2, 1928, means that she was a participant in the transitional period for the Whitney on a large scale, significant to the history of Wilhelmina Weber, the modernist and to the museum as we see it today.

Thomas Furlong, 3 Washington Square, ca. 1924

While in New York City, Thomas Furlong wrote frequent editorials at the request of the Nation Editorial Staff, and Wilhelmina Weber entertained their employees in 1919 over two evenings. "The Nation," which is one of the oldest weekly Magazines in America, had a strong relationship with Thomas. "The Nation" staff called Wilhelmina Weber "Miss Weber" in 1919, after she had married Thomas Furlong. Calling attention to the fact his wife was well-liked by many, she often became the topic of interest, most always earning mention of her endearing qualities. Those who corresponded with the couple would repeatedly quote something she loved. People just seemed to remember his wife.

"The Nation" correspondence note refers to Cecil Crawford O'Gorman (1874-1943), the son of Irish immigrants and a noted painter and mining engineer from Mexico, whose son was the architect and accomplished Mexican muralist Juan O'Gorman (1905-1982). This "Nation" correspondence evidently was the request of more than just chance meeting. After their return from Mexico five years earlier, O' Gorman visited Wilhelmina Weber and Thomas Furlong at Golden Heart, where they received a pencil drawing from O' Gorman. This interesting letter reveals the "Nation" editor was asking Thomas to look into the art of a rather "strange man" who wanted his pictures published in the "Nation." There was a traveling show at the League Galleries where the works of O'Gorman were on display at that time. The artist years later established him-self by painting the murals of the UNAM Central Library of Mexico City and the mural in library Gertrudis Bocanegra in Pátzcuaro, Michoacán Mexico.

The Nation, 20 Vesey Street (P. O. Box 794).

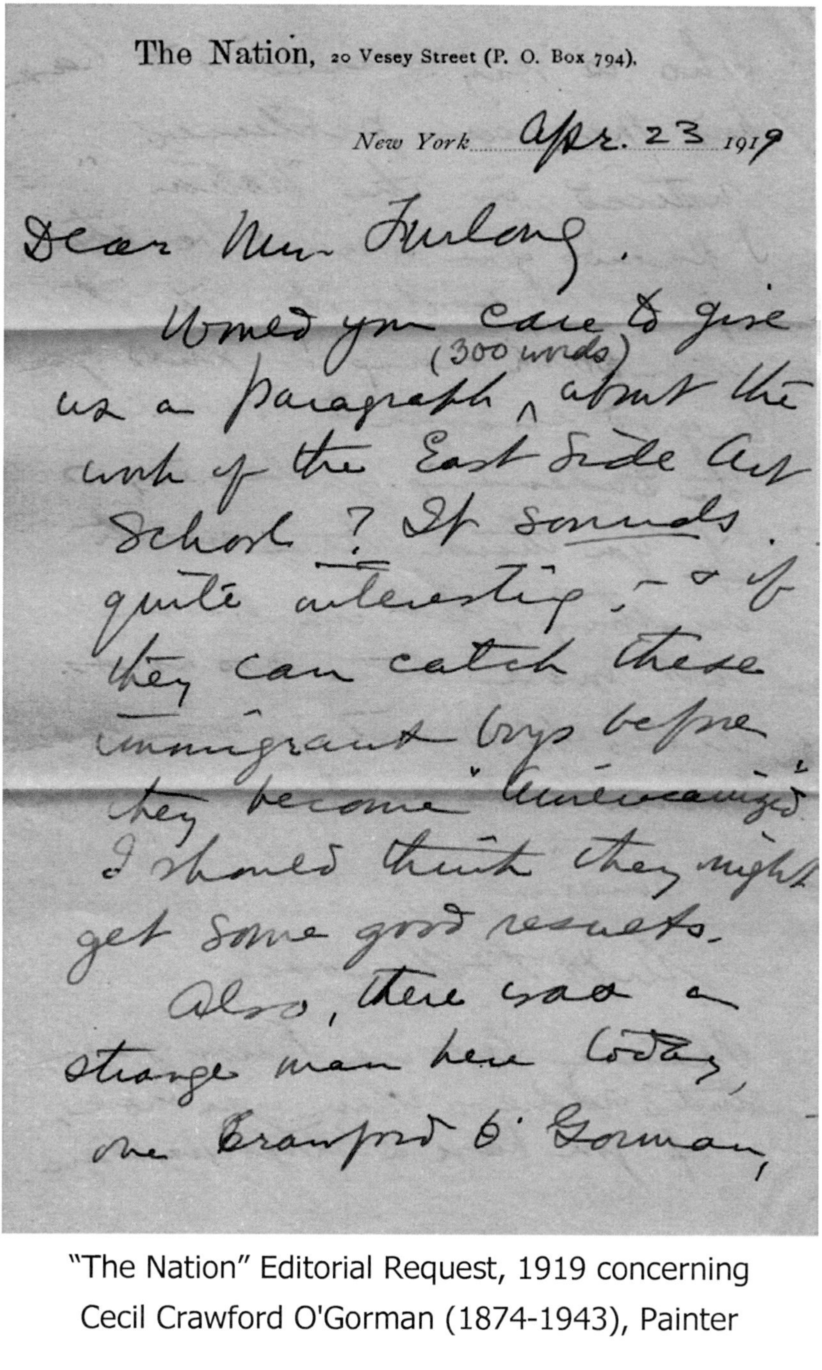

New York Apr. 23 1919

Dear Mr. Furlong.

Would you care to give us a paragraph (300 words) about the work of the East Side Art School? It sounds quite interesting, — & if they can catch these immigrant boys before they become "Americanized" I should think they might get some good results.

Also, there was a strange man here today, one Crawford O'Gorman,

"The Nation" Editorial Request, 1919 concerning
Cecil Crawford O'Gorman (1874-1943), Painter

who is very anxious to have
his Mexican pictures
noticed in the "Nation" —
I knew you would be the
person to do it, if it
were worth doing! Would you
be good enough to look in at
the Dudensing galleries, —
if you think them worth
anything, let us have
not more than 300 words.
Unless the paintings are more
desirable than the man ___!

Sincerely

W. H. B. Mussey

Please let us know your
studio address when you move,
— if you have a telephone there.

"The Nation" Editorial Request, 1919 (cont)

The Nation

20 Vesey Street, New York

March 22, 1919.

Mr. Tomás Furlong,
    41 Commerce St.,
        New York, N. Y.

My dear Mr. Furlong:

    . Thank you for your very satisfactory editorial paragraph on Mr. Cox which I am very glad indeed to have for next week's Nation. It was very kind of you to get your friend to bring it in promptly.

    Please tell Miss Webber how much the Nation staff are enjoying her hospitality. The office has been full of remarks concerning the pleasantness of the two evenings we have spent with you.

                    Very sincerely yours,

                    H.R.Mussey

                            Managing Editor.

"The Nation" memo, 1919 concerning
Kenyon Cox (1856-1919)

This particular "Nation" editorial request to Thomas Furlong referred to the passing of Kenyon Cox (October 27, 1856 – March 17, 1919), who died at the age of 62. Mr. Cox was a very important early instructor at the Art Students League, a painter, muralist, illustrator, teacher, and writer. He designed the League's logo and motto "Nulla Dies Sine Linea - No Day without a Line." Kenyon Cox and Thomas had worked together as muralists, offering each other their support, as they were both accomplished New

York muralists. Kenyon Cox also spent a great deal of time in Paris from 1877 to 1882, where he followed the trends of the time, and he felt a new wave of enlightenment and painting was under way. Kenyon was very much an intellectual who was not so much emboldened by the new trends that were emerging at that time with the modernism movement.

Thomas wrote for the "New York Globe" At that time, the Globe was going strong. Revamped in 1904, it was now a penny paper. It would seem Mr. Furlong had become an art critic at large for the paper, and the friendship with the editor was a bond from New York City that came about after meeting at the Art Students League. Thomas Furlong maintained a lasting relationship with the newspaper.

Thomas Furlong's Grant Proposal

We know that Thomas Furlong applied to the Guggenheim for an art studies fellowship grant to study in Europe. Fortunately, they returned the résumé for us to discover in a letter from them postmarked December 2, 1927. It was another professor, John Wesley Carroll at NYU, who received the fellowship. We can understand much from a person's life if we look at the successes and the rejections one encounters along the road to accomplishment. The process continues throughout the lifetime of people who are noteworthy and at some point, they leave something behind that we might discover to complete the journey. What they have left behind might one day contribute to our great society. The important Guggenheim grant letter reveals the close professional tie to Rockwell Kent that Thomas and Weber Furlong had for many years.

The study proposal to the Guggenheim is quite revealing it shows his deep devotion to mural studies and to the great masters. Explained further with some detail in this direct quote from Thomas, in which he states his intent concerning the grant application, as follows:

Statement of Study Plan

"As little wet fresco Mural Decorations in the Antique method or style is being done today in America, and as there are no places known to me in this country where one can investigate and study the same, and as there is a very definite school at Fontainebleau, France with a Wet Fresco Class under the direction of Mrs. Baudoin and St. Hubert. I should like to take with me an original design as large as practicable to work out in full under the direction of these artists at Fontainebleau.   Following this practical period of study, which would consume approximately three months,   I should like to study the works of the great masters of the past in Painting, Sculpture and decoration as well as those of note today, as follows:

France

Fontainebleau, Paris, the great Cathedral town, Chateaux and Provence.

Italy

Florence, Siena, Assisi, Padua, Arezzo, Rome, Venice, Ravena, Pompeii. (Sicily 12 Century Mosaics and Tunis for Mosaic floors)

Spain

Catalonia for the Primitifs; Madrid for the Prado, Toledo for El Greco, Sevilla for Primitifs, Saint Sejo de Copostello for its Porta de la Floria, Monastery of Guadeloupe for its vestments.

Belgium

Flemish School Ghent, Bruges, Antwerp and Brussels

England

The Great Galleries of London if possible

"The Purpose of the study plan is to incorporate into my own work the inspiration which comes from association of great things. To see, to learn, to appreciate all that I feel worthwhile and to cheerfully discard all befogged traditions. I fully expect the result of my plan will appear in all paintings I may do while in Europe upon my return and in my future teaching."

In the following communication, the Post Impressionist painter Allen Tucker (1866-1939) sends his Good Luck wishes along with the final copy of the plan of study concerning the Guggenheim fellowship Thomas Furlong had sought. The two were close friends and maintained a professional relationship. Tucker would visit Golden Heart between 1921 and 1931. This is only my conjecture and I am sure in the future, a conclusion waits. This is not the only item open to discussion from Golden Heart, only adding mystery to the Treasured Collection of Golden Heart Farm.

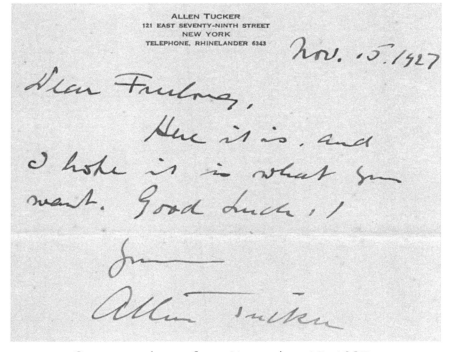

Correspondence from November 15, 1927

This is signifcant to the Allen Tucker Foundation

By the 1930s, things were going pretty well for Thomas Furlong and Wilhelmina Weber. They had expanded the farm another eighty acres, bringing the total acreage to one-hundred-eighty, after purchase of the neighboring farm of Harry and George Wright for $900.00, with a $20 deposit. It included additional barns and the farmhouse adjacent to Golden Heart. Mina Myers Wilhelmina's cousin purchased part of this parcel of land. Her cabin remains to this day.

September 29. 1930.

Received from Wilhelmina Weber Furlong and Thomas Furlong 20⁰⁰ toward the first payment on farm of 80 acres = for 900.⁰⁰ _____

Harry Wright.

George Wright

Their teaching was paying off, and Golden Heart was busy with students and accomplished artists enjoying the countryside and painting on the mountaintop. They both had achieved popularity within their communities, and they were actively painting themselves. The two retained a residence in New York for many years and a summer home in the popular Bolton Landing landscape.

Thomas at The Golden Heart Art Barn, ca. 1939

Bernard E. Weber III Continues the Journey

Bernard Erwin Weber III (1928-1990) at Golden Heart
Farm, back entrance, 1940

My father would come to Golden Heart Farm just prior to
1936, at a time when things were at their best for the Furlongs. Since they had no children, they enjoyed the opportunity to have their young nephew Ben visit. During his
time at the farm, Weber tasked him with keeping the water
supply full at the farmhouse and when people were staying
at the Little Houses, he would fetch water for the artists
using one of the many enamel buckets that could be found
throughout the farm. In 1969, He told a story of the numerous broken glass pitchers on the road to the creek and
we were fortunate to discover some of them during the
filming this year of our documentary some seventy-six
years later. His Aunt Wilhelmina and Uncle Thomas wrote
about him often and always kept his photograph on display
at Golden Heart Farm. After Wilhelmina Weber Furlong's
mother and father passed away, her brother Bernard We-

ber purchased a house on Mulberry St. in San Antonio, Texas in the early 1930's; well before World War II. Wilhelmina Weber Furlong and Thomas Furlong visited her brother and sister-in-law in Texas usually in the winter around the Christmas holidays. My grandmother, Jean J. Weber visited Golden Heart Farm bringing my dad with her to stay until winter. Wilhelmina Weber Furlong's brother, Bernard Weber was my father's great-grandfather and Weber Furlong was his grand Aunt. My father Ben divided his time between San Antonio and Bolton Landing, New York in the spring and summer months, spending winter at home in Texas. She and her husband Thomas Furlong visited them on many occasions during dad's early childhood before the death of his father. After Thomas passed away, Mina Meyer would drive Wilhelmina Weber to San Antonio for the winter holidays.

Wilhelmina Weber Furlong did paint on her early visits to San Antonio, Texas, however, we do not know exactly which paintings with the Mexican influence of San Antonio are attributed to her visits. San Antonio, Texas to Weber Furlong represented southern Mexico, which is a defined period of her artwork beginning in 1906 and ending 1913 with her departure from Mexico. However, she painted later works representing Mexico ending about 1949. Because of these visits to San Antonio, she continued to paint works representing her love of Old Mexico

Bernard E. Weber III served in the U.S. Air Force from 1949 to 1959, and rose to the rank of Major in the reserves. He earned a B.S. degree in Civil Engineering from the University of Texas at Austin in 1955. He was a consulting engineer before going to work for 3M Company from 1956 to 1986. Wilhelmina Weber only visited us once in San Antonio in 1962. However, during the years her brother operated the French Bootery Company, she would visit him more often.

Her story continues now with the traveling Wilhelmina Weber Furlong Exhibition, "The Treasured Collection" of Golden Heart Farm, and the Wilhelmina Weber Furlong Foundation. We now have a much better picture of the great early American Modern Artist Wilhelmina Weber, as well as the woman, in all her grandeur, with her flowing heavy cotton dark work dress common to women in the 1890s.

Today, if you were to walk past her successful gallery (from 1913 to 1924) on 122 East 59th Street, New York City, you would find the old painted red brick building still standing. Originally white brick, the entrance remains. This is where much of her New York City life had begun. There was an upstairs apartment and a storefront down below. In 2011, it was a nutrition center (you can view the image on Google Earth). Furthermore, Wilhelmina Weber's prestigious 3 Washington Square address is a popular New York University history walk and museum for Edward Hopper, well-known for the secret passage to his studio. This is one of the city's most important notable locations, for not only was it the studio of the artist Edward Hopper, but also the studio of America's first woman modernist painter. A most important historical detail for New York University made even more significant to the people of New York City today. In that light, we must consider that more of the story is yet to be told. Interesting facts surround this amazing woman.

Golden Heart farmhouse still stands as a testament to Wilhelmina Weber's life at the artist colony in Bolton Landing. The Little Houses, once in an open field, still stand, in an overgrown forest, almost entirely in ruin. However, two remain, surviving the test of time. The entrance to the farm has moved. The old road into the farm is overgrown, but still traversable. The modern world has not completely taken over. One still gets a sense of the story that unfolded here as one walks the grounds.

"Saint Swithin's Tool House", 2012
Courtesy of Ted Caldwell of Bolton Landing

In this photo, we see the stunning but quaint Little House called "Saint Swithin's Tool House," home to some of the greatest art figures of the Modern Art movement; its inhabitants escaping New York City to expand their horizons were profoundly affected by its serenity. Great works of American art and poetry were created here only a stone's throw from the main farmhouse between 1921 and 1960. Among its inhabitants were John Graham, Dorothy Dehner, and David Smith. George Barber clarified its history in January of 2013 during an interview with Clint Weber for the "In Search of Weber" film project. Without Mr. Barber's insight into the life of Weber Furlong, some of the personal side to Golden Heart Farm would have been lost.

Remaining "Little House" with loft, 2012
Courtesy of Ted Caldwell of Bolton Landing

Completely re-done shortly after purchasing the farm in 1921 the lofted "Little House" was another favorite of Wilhelmina Weber further from the main farmhouse it boasted a private matching privy. It was originally a small log cabin built after the Civil War by the farms original owners, more than likely as a place to live while the main farmhouse was being constructed. The Furlongs added a loft and planked siding, which the couple painted red with a heavy pigment wash. The insides of all the Little Houses were quaint and well-furnished, with painted highlights and wood burning stoves. This Little House featured a single seated outhouse nearby that has totally collapsed. It in addition was painted red.

Golden Heart in 2012
Courtesy of Ted Caldwell of Bolton Landing

A concise history of Golden Heart Farm, described in 1961 in the Thursday, November 16, edition of "The Warrensburg News," provides its whole story:

"Romance and history surround three old Bolton Landing Homes described as follows"

"The third old house is located high on Federal Hill, south of the Sagamore Golf Club, with one of the most magnificent views of the lake in the vicinity. This ground-hugging farmhouse was built after the Civil War. The builder was Rufus Randall, one of the three sons of Abel Randall who during the war had built what is now known as the Maranville home on Valley Road. When Rufus and his brother returned from the war, the young men set about establishing homes. After the family was raised, Mr. Randall sold to Edson Pearson who lived with his family in the home many years. Eventually Thomas Furlong and Wilhelmina Weber came into possession of the property. At this time, the character of the property changed from farming to an art colony for Mr. and Mrs. Furlong were both distinguished painters. Recently the property was sold to Michael Dreyfus who has known and loved the place for many years. Here then, are the stories of the Vandenburg, the Goldman Organ Factory and the Randall-Furlong homes. Prospects for the continued usefulness of the two are bright; the third seems to have completed its term of service."

Original Golden Heart Farm front entrance in 2012
Courtesy of Ted Caldwell of Bolton Landing

Perhaps of greatest significance is the strong attachment the communities of Bolton landing and Glens Falls still hold for the Weber Furlongs' great place in American art history. Both communities have dedicated resources to preserving this story. Local Bolton Landing town historians and grand international museums hold the works of Wilhelmina Weber, Dorothy Dehner, and David Smith, both her close and dear friends held in high regard. The final Wilhelmina Weber studio gallery in downtown Glens Falls remains, the place where she left this world. The place we know is witness to her life and the continuation of this final chapter. The story is real, the places are real, and the people involved lived the life, during a great and difficult time.

The End

Afterword

We now come to the end of the fabulous story about the multifaceted journey of two great early American Modern Artists who lived life so well, a continuation of their legacy through our study and celebration of their life together. From the late 1890s and on into the early 1950s, their love story continued and grew, all the way through two world wars, a revolution in Mexico, international travel, and intrigue, and friendships and studies with some of the greatest artists the world had to offer.

They loved and lived life boldly and completely, while honoring and celebrating the simplicity of life. When I think of the lives of Wilhelmina Weber and her beloved Thomas, I am overcome with a great sense of joy and accomplishment as I understand and appreciate two remarkable human beings in America's early art movements.

The survival of the many items in the Weber Furlong Collection is the marvel of this project. In them, a story has emerged. People's lives and a great historic place are now better defined. I can only hope, in the rush to get the story told for the exhibition, we have not missed important facts or history that needs mention. The immensely popular and well-liked New York woman and her beloved Thomas has simply been hidden away, but not entirely forgotten.

One hundred and thirty five years later, this story that spans three generations and the small boy who admired wonderful art in private can inspire future generations, as we celebrate a great woman, her devoted husband and colleague, and their beloved Golden Heart Farm, their legacy a gift to the world and to us as well.

Special Thanks

Special thanks to the collaborative efforts of Mitzi Weber Royer, for her firsthand experiences with Wilhelmina Weber Furlong and to Professor Emeritus James K. Kettewell, of Skidmore College, for graciously providing his essay on my great aunt. As he said, "I was always concerned about what had happened to her work. All I remember, if I remember correctly, is that a Glens Falls art dealer named Thur Krarup had rolled her canvases up, and had sent them to her heirs in Texas."

Professor James Kettlewell and Clint Weber
"In Search of Weber" Field Trip
Golden Heart Farm, 2012

Professor James Kettlewell, Sam Caldwell, Ted Caldwell, Jessica Rubin, and Mona Blocker Garcia

"In Search of Weber" Field Trip, 2012

Weber's Broken Water Pitcher 2012
(described by Bernard E. Weber III in 1969)

Bolton Landing, New York

We especially thank the citizens of Bolton Landing and of Glens Falls for the support and hard work they put forth to help make the project a successful event for the communities involved. We would like to thank the Hyde Collection in Glens Falls for the effort they put forth with assisting us with research material and for a special viewing of their Weber and Furlong paintings. We are very greatful to Anthony and Lisa Hall of the "Lake George Mirror" for their gift to the Weber Furlong Collection of mural prints and graphic designs by Thomas Furlong, and to Ted Caldwell, Bolton Landing's official town historian who planned the Bolton Landing segment of the "In Search of Weber" field trip project.

Special Thanks and Credits

Jim Royer and Mitzi Royer

Wilhelmina Weber Furlong

Thomas Furlong

Rodolfo Garcia and Mona Blocker Garcia

James Kettlewell

Rebecca Smith

George Barber and Eileen Allen

Katie DeGroot

Mayor Jack Diamond City of Glens Falls,New York

Wayne Wright Historian City of Glens Falls

Erin Coe The Hyde Collection Glens Falls,New York

Bernard R. Brown

Loren Blackburn

Ted and Jane Caldwell

Henry Caldwell

Theta Swinton Curri

Rosemary Kingsley

Cathy DeDe "The Chronicle" Glens Falls, New York

Meredith Thomas

Nanson Serrianne

Edmund Rucinski

Charles Peveto

Doug Deneen, Trees Bookstore Bolton Landing

Barbara Edwards

Art Students League of New York

Special Thanks and Credits

Bolton Landing Historical Society
Town of Bolton Landing
Bolton Landing Chamber Of Commerce
Post Star Glens Falls, New York
Press Republican Plattsburgh, New York
Lake George Mirror
Warrensburg, NY Lake George News
International Woman's Foundation, Studio 98 Marfa, Texas
Schenectady Gazette
Dorothy Zelazny Angrist
Elinor Elliott
Raphael Colb
Rodney Congdon
Ralph Russo
Chuck Stephenson
Allison Scott
Susan Brink
Rebecca Garza
Marfa Rotary Club
Shirly Biellier, Alpine Picture Framing
The Sagamore Hotel
Arcon Inn Marfa, Texas
Marfa Chamber of Commerce
Look TV Glens Falls, New York
North Country Public Radio

Weber Furlong A Retrospective

"Weber Furlong" a retrospective is the first major exhibition in Marfa, Texas devoted to one of the most important woman painters of the early twentieth-century, Wilhelmina Weber Furlong (1878-1962). The Retrospective features paintings and archival items that span the entirety of the artist's celebrated life. The groundbreaking exhibition and its accompanying documentary film "In Search of Weber" and catalogue bring together the most significant works from Wilhelmina Weber's career. Included are prolific paintings, personal effects, and photographs. It is the most comprehensive examination to date of Wilhelmina Weber's work a re-evaluation of the artist's work in light of her prominent place as a woman in early Modern American Art.

Marfa, Texas is the venue for this exhibition, which draws from the artist's private collection and personal belongings. Marfa, Texas, was selected because the artist Donald Judd was a student at the Art Students League in 1948, and Wilhelmina Weber, who pioneered this unique community shared the close relationships of Modern Artists in the movement. We can experience the beginning and the end of a great and diverse time for American Modernism.

WILHELMINA WEBER FURLONG

THE GRAND RETROSPECTIVE   SEPTEMBER 27 - NOVEMBER 15, 2012

America's first woman modern artist and the Treasured Collection of Golden Heart Farm

BUILDING 98 Marfa, Texas   The International Woman's Foundation

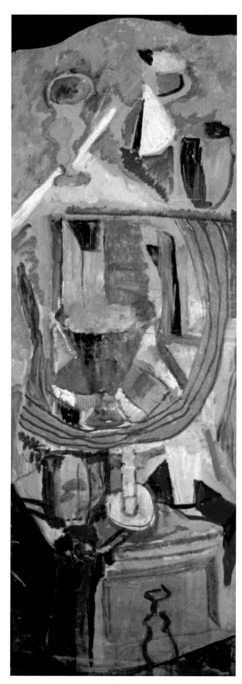

Triptych Mural, Ca 1899-1906

Title "Winter" Lake George landscape Golden Heart Farm
1923

"Water Mark" Weber Mexico, 1906-1913

Glens Falls, 1947-1955

New York, 1915-1921

New York 1913-1920

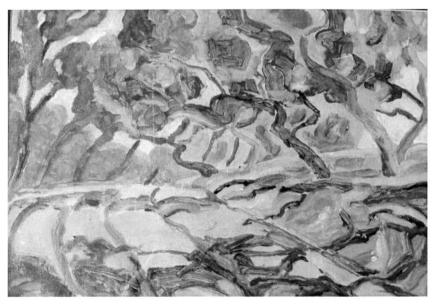

Paris, 1903-1906

Original Folio Paris, 1899-1906

Original Folio Paris, 1899-1906

Paris 1899-1906

Mexico 1907

Golden Heart, 1928-1930

Painted on a dish towel during the Great Depression

Corner of the towel

Golden Heart, 1945-1950

Mexico, 1906-1911

Hallway-Golden Heart, 1936-1940

Glens Falls, 1952-1957

Golden Heart, 1945-1948

New York, 1914-1923

Golden Heart, 1939-1947

St. Louis 1921-1927

Golden Heart, 1921-1929

Mexico, 1906-1913

Golden Heart 1920-1927

Golden Heart, 1952-1957

Mexico, 1906-1912

Golden Heart, 1948-1955

Mexico, 1906-1912

New York, 1939-1945

Mexico City, 1906-1907

Glens Falls, 1960-1962

Glens Falls, 1957-1960

Mexico, 1906-1912

Golden Heart, 1931

Golden Heart 1921-1929

Bolton Landing 1921-1929

St. Louis 1897-1902

New York, Minimalism 1952-1955

Saint Swithin's Tool House, 1923

New York 1897-1903

Paris, 1898-1903

Paris, 1903-1906

Glens Falls, 1957

Glens Falls, 1961-1962

New York 1918-1923

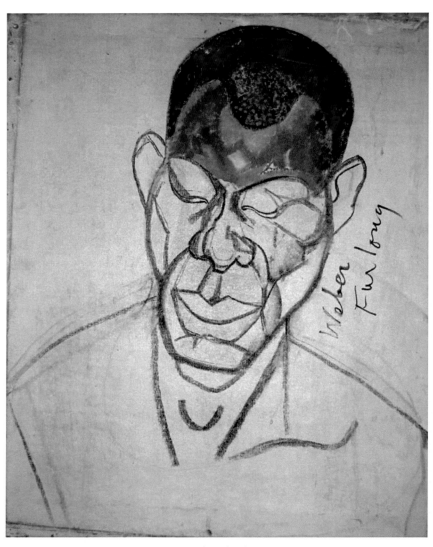

New York 1919-1925

During the Harlem Renaissance

Early modern work New York, 1914-1923

The Ostrich Egg New York, 1923-1931

John Graham, 1927

Chicago Thomas Furlong, 1925-1935

John Graham's portrait of Wilhelmina Weber

1921-1925

Paris, Minimalism John Graham, 1928

Portrait of Wilhelmina by Thomas Furlong, ca 1911-1912

Reverse Side Weber 1913-1917

Map of Bolton Landing, New York

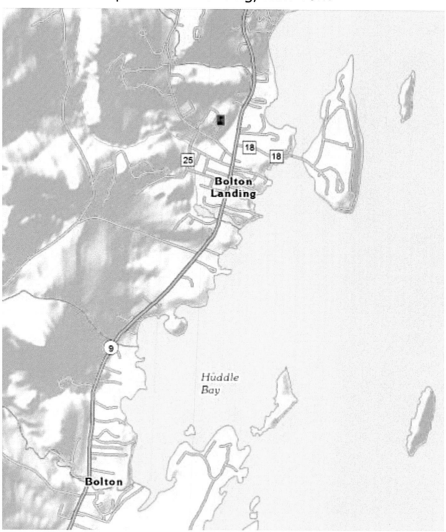

Courtesy of the National Map

Map of Glens Falls, New York

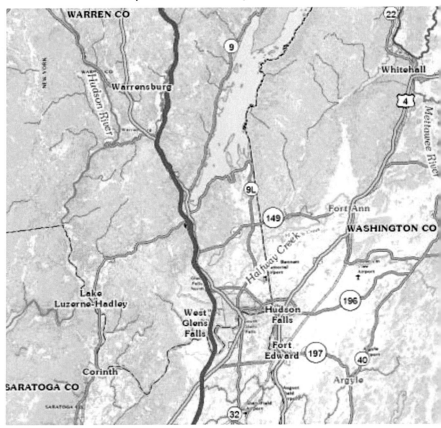

Courtesy of the National Map

Rough Outline of Golden Heart 1926

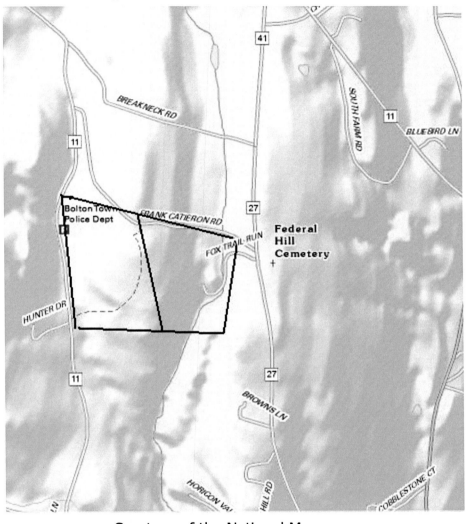

Courtesy of the National Map

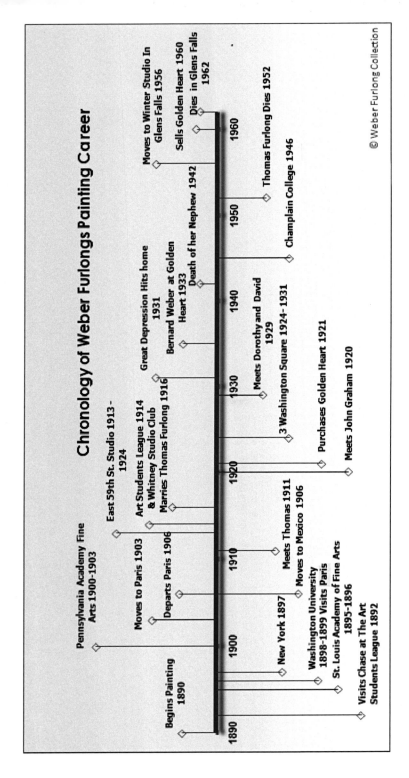

Chronology of Weber Furlongs Painting Career

- Begins Painting 1890
- Visits Chase at The Art Students League 1892
- St. Louis Academy of Fine Arts 1895-1896
- New York 1897
- Washington University 1898-1899 Visits Paris
- Pennsylvania Academy Fine Arts 1900-1903
- Moves to Paris 1903
- Departs Paris 1906
- Moves to Mexico 1906
- Meets Thomas 1911
- East 59th St. Studio 1913 - 1924
- Art Students League 1914 & Whitney Studio Club
- Marries Thomas Furlong 1916
- Meets John Graham 1920
- Purchases Golden Heart 1921
- 3 Washington Square 1924-1931
- Meets Dorothy and David 1929
- Great Depression Hits home 1931
- Bernard Weber at Golden Heart 1933
- Death of her Nephew 1942
- Champlain College 1946
- Thomas Furlong Dies 1952
- Moves to Winter Studio In Glens Falls 1956
- Sells Golden Heart 1960
- Dies in Glens Falls 1962

1890 1900 1910 1920 1930 1940 1950 1960